THE POCKET IDIOT'S GUIDE TO

Vitamins

D1560359

by Alan H. Pressman, D.C., Ph.D., C.C.N., and Sheila Buff

alpha books

Macmillan USA, Inc.
201 West 103rd Street
Indianapolis, IN 46290

A Pearson Education Company

Alpha Development Team

Publisher
Marie Butler-Knight

Editorial Director
Gary M. Krebs

Associate Managing Editor
Cari Shaw Fischer

Acquisitions Editors
Amy Gordon
Randy Ladenheim-Gil

Development Editors
Phil Kitchel
Amy Zavatto

Assistant Editor
Georgette Blau

Production Team

Development Editor
Joan D. Paterson

Production Editor
Christy Wagner

Cover Designer
Mike Freeland

Photo Editor
Richard H. Fox

Illustrator
Jody P. Schaeffer

Book Designers
Scott Cook and Amy Adams of DesignLab

Indexer
Brad Herriman

Layout/Proofreading
Angela Calvert
Mary Hunt

Contents

Introduction

Every year Americans spend more than $4 *billion* on vitamins, minerals, and other supplements. Why? They're seeking better health, a longer, more vigorous life, or maybe just help for a painful health problem. Are they finding it? Yes! Can you? Yes! If you understand how important vitamins and minerals are, and what they can—and can't—do. You, too, can achieve better health.

This book is a concise guide to understanding vitamins and minerals. We wrote it to give you straight answers about nutritional supplements, based on real research, not hype. We believe that reading this book will help you make the right choices for you.

Why Are They So Important?

You need 13 different vitamins and at least 10 minerals to stay alive. Vitamins and minerals are essential to your health—you have to have them. They're needed to make the thousands of enzymes, hormones, and other chemical messengers your body uses to grow, repair itself, make energy, remove wastes, defend you against infection, and generally keep you running smoothly. You also need them to keep your bones strong, your eyes sharp, and your brain alert. And most important of all, you need them to help protect you against cancer and heart disease.

The *only* way you can get all those vitamins and minerals into your body is to eat them. That's why we'll talk about your diet over and over again in this book—the foods you eat are your best way to get the nutrients you need. But even if you could eat right all the time—and most people can't—you might still benefit from some extra vitamins and minerals.

Do You Really Need Vitamin Pills?

The short answer is yes—the long answers are found in each chapter of this book. Try as we might, most of us just can't eat a good, nutritious diet at every meal every day. We need the help vitamin and mineral supplements can give. And sometimes we need a vitamin or mineral boost to help deal with health problems. The amounts we need are more than we could reasonably get from our food. Finally, some vitamins, like vitamin E, are most valuable in large doses—doses far greater (though very safe) than the amounts you could ever get from your food only.

Taking supplements can improve your health now and insure it for the future. Supplements are an easy, safe, and inexpensive way to make sure you're getting the vitamins and minerals your body has to have for optimum health.

Throughout this book, we give you useful information and tips in sidebars. Here's what the different sidebars are all about:

What's in a Word?

These sidebars expand the definitions of special terms and basic concepts.

Now You're Cooking

Here you'll find tips on how to get the most from your foods and supplements.

Quack, Quack

We also have a special sidebar reserved for exploding some of the sillier ideas about supplements. These boxes help you avoid supplements that don't work.

Trademarks

All terms mentioned in this book that are known to be or are suspected of being trademarks or service marks have been appropriately capitalized. Alpha Books and Macmillan USA, Inc. cannot attest to the accuracy of this information. Use of a term in this book should not be regarded as affecting the validity of any trademark or service mark.

Chapter 1

The A to K of Nutrition

In This Chapter

➤ Why you need vitamins and minerals

➤ How much do you need?

➤ Vitamins, minerals, and your diet

➤ How vitamins and minerals protect you from damaging free radicals

➤ Interpreting the Recommended Dietary Allowance (RDA)

➤ What's right for you?

Walk into any health-food store or drugstore and you're faced with shelf after shelf crammed with vitamins, minerals, and supplements of all sorts. What is all this stuff? How can you choose? What's best for *you*?

To decide wisely for your health, you need to understand what each vitamin does—and why you need them *all*. You need to understand what minerals do for you—and why you need them *all*. You need to understand how the vitamins and minerals in your food affect you—and how everything else in your food affects you as well. You need to understand which of those other supplements are valuable to your health—and which aren't.

Although all those bottles on the shelves may seem confusing and a little scary, they're really not. Once you understand the easy basics of vitamins and minerals, you'll be able to pick the supplements that will help *your* health.

Vitamins: Why They're Vital

A vitamin is an organic (carbon-containing) chemical compound your body must have in very small amounts for normal growth, metabolism (creating energy in your cells), and health. You need vitamins to make *enzymes* and *hormones*—important substances your body uses to make all the many chemical reactions you need to live. You *must* get your vitamins from your food or from supplements—you can't make them in your body.

What's in a Word?

Enzymes are chemical compounds your body makes from various combinations of proteins, vitamins, and minerals. Enzymes speed up chemical reactions in your body. **Hormones** are chemical messengers your body makes to tell your organs what to do. Hormones regulate many activities, including your growth, blood pressure, heart rate, glucose levels, and sexual characteristics.

There are 13 vitamins in all, and you need every single one of them, no exceptions. Vitamins aren't food or a substitute for food. They have no calories and give you no energy directly—but your body needs vitamins, especially the B vitamins, to convert food to energy. We'll look at each vitamin in detail in the later chapters of this book, but for now we'll divide them into two groups: *fat-soluble* and *water-soluble*.

Fat-Soluble Vitamins

Fat-soluble vitamins are stored in your body, mostly in your fatty tissues and in your liver. Vitamins A, E, D, and K are fat-soluble—that is, they dissolve in fat but not water. Because you can store these vitamins, you don't have to get a supply of them every day. On the other hand, getting too much of these vitamins means they could build up in your body and cause problems.

Water-Soluble Vitamins

Water-soluble vitamins can't really be stored in your body for very long. That's because these vitamins dissolve in water, so any extra is carried out of your body. Vitamin C and all the B vitamins are water-soluble. Because you can't store these vitamins, you need to get a fresh supply every day. You can't really overdose on water-soluble vitamins. Unless you take truly massive doses, the extra just washes harmlessly out.

How Much Do You Need?

How much you need of each vitamin is a question that has a lot of different answers, depending on who you are and who you ask. For now, we're going to tell you what the doctors and scientists at the Food and Nutrition Board of the Institute of Medicine, a division of the National Academy of Science, think is enough to meet your basic needs for each vitamin, assuming you're an average healthy adult man or woman. The Institute of Medicine is the group that brings you the Recommended Dietary Allowances, better known as RDAs. (We'll talk a lot more about RDAs and other ways of looking at your vitamin and mineral needs in the next chapter.) Check out the chart on the inside front cover of this book to see the RDAs for vitamins. These are the *minimum* amounts you

should be getting every day, preferably from your food
(and from vitamin pills if you need them).

Quack, Quack

The only thing a vitamin can cure is a deficiency disease
caused by a shortage of that vitamin. Vitamin C cures
scurvy but not the common cold, although it can shorten
its duration. Vitamins in amounts larger than the RDA can
help prevent or treat health problems, not cure them.

Beyond the Basics

Throughout this book, we'll use the RDA as the rock-
bottom, bare minimum amount you need to get every
day for a particular vitamin or mineral. That's because the
RDAs are only the amounts needed to prevent disease in
ordinary healthy people. They are, in our opinion and the
opinion of many other nutritionists, doctors, and researchers, the *least* you should get. (In fairness, we should
say that the Institute of Medicine is looking carefully at
the current RDAs and will probably revise some of them
upward over the next few years.) In many cases, we believe the RDAs are far from the amount you need to reach
optimal good health or to prevent many serious health
problems, like heart disease. As you'll discover in the
chapters to come, there are many, many good reasons for
taking more—sometimes much more—than the RDA.
There are also sometimes many good reasons to stick to
the RDA and *not* take any extra—and we'll cover those issues as well.

Minerals: Essential Elements of Health

A *mineral* is an inorganic chemical element, such as calcium or potassium, that your body must have in very small amounts for normal growth, metabolism, and health and to make many enzymes and hormones. Like vitamins, you must get your minerals from your food.

We use the word mineral in a broad sense to mean all the many inorganic substances you need every day, but we should really be a little more exact. Nutritionally speaking, a mineral is an inorganic substance that you need every day in amounts over 100 milligrams (mg). If you need less than 100 mg a day, we call the mineral a *trace mineral* or *trace element*. Even though the amounts you need for a trace mineral are very small—sometimes no more than 50 micrograms (mcg)—they're just as important to your health as the major minerals.

Minerals

The minerals you need every day include calcium, chloride, magnesium, phosphorus, potassium, and sodium. We deal with these all in separate chapters (potassium, sodium, and chloride are combined in Chapter 11, "Electrolytes: The Elements of Good Health"). Take a look at the chart on the inside back cover of this book to see the RDAs for the major minerals.

Now You're Cooking

A lot of the vitamins in fruits and vegetables are lost between the farm and your plate. The longer the foods are stored before you eat them, the more nutrients are lost. Heat, light, and exposure to air all reduce the amount of vitamins, especially vitamin C, thiamin, and folic acid.

Trace Minerals

How many trace elements you need to get and in what amounts is open to a lot of discussion (see Chapter 12, "The Trace Minerals: A Little Goes a Long Way"). We know for sure that you need very small amounts of boron, chromium, cobalt, copper, iodine, iron, manganese, molybdenum, nickel, selenium, silicon, tin, vanadium, and zinc. What about the tiny, tiny amounts of other minerals, like aluminum and lithium, that are found in your body? We don't really know why you have them or how much you need.

A lot of the trace minerals don't have RDAs—we just don't know enough to set any. Your need for boron, for example, was only discovered in the mid-1980s, and researchers are still trying to figure what the RDA should be. Instead, some of these minerals have Safe and Adequate Intakes (SAIs). These are best guesses as to how much you probably need. They're often given as a fairly broad range. For example, the SAI for chromium seems to be anywhere from 50 to 200 mcg. The chart on the inside back cover lists the RDAs and SAIs for the trace minerals that have them—we've left off the ones that don't.

Do You Need Vitamin and Mineral Supplements?

The average person can get the RDAs for vitamins and minerals simply by eating a reasonable diet containing plenty of whole grains and fresh fruits and vegetables. Yeah, right. First of all, who's that mythical average person? Not anyone we know. The RDAs assume you're an adult under age 60 who's in good health, has perfect digestion, isn't overweight, leads a totally stress-free life, doesn't ever have any sort of medical problem, and never needs to take any sort of medicine. The RDAs also assume that you really manage to eat a good diet every day.

Let's get real here: Even on a good day, you can't always manage a completely healthful diet. Who has the time or energy to do all that shopping and food preparation? On any given day, half of us eat at least one meal away from home anyway. You just can't always eat healthfully, even when you try.

The fact is, most of us don't try all that hard, and most of us don't meet all the RDAs from our diet. According to the results of the 1994 Department of Agriculture's Continuing Survey of Food Intakes by Individuals (CSFII):

➤ Most adult women don't meet the RDAs for iron, zinc, vitamin B_6 (pyridoxine), calcium, magnesium, and vitamin E.

➤ Most adult men don't meet the RDA for zinc and magnesium.

➤ Young children drink 16 percent less milk than they did in the late 1970s, but they drink 23 percent more carbonated soft drinks.

➤ Americans eat very few dark-green leafy vegetables and deep-yellow vegetables. Fewer than one out of five people eats five fresh fruits and vegetables a day—and about one person in five doesn't eat any.

If it's that hard to meet the RDAs through diet, what about reaching the higher amounts of vitamins and minerals many health professionals now recommend? You could just try harder to eat better or differently. For example, women between the ages of 25 and 50 should get at least 1,000 mg of calcium every day to keep their bones strong. That's the calcium in three glasses of milk a day. You could easily drink that much milk, but would you? Do you even like milk? What if you hate the stuff or have trouble digesting it?

One of the biggest problems with the RDAs is that they assume you're in good health and eat about 2,000 calories a day. What if you don't eat that much? Many people over age 70, for example, only take in about 1,500 calories a day. And in our weight-conscious society, at any given time one in six Americans is dieting—usually in a way that doesn't provide good nutrition. There's no way these people are getting the vitamins and minerals they need from their food.

We'd be the first to tell you that vitamin and mineral supplements aren't a substitute for healthy eating. They're also not a magic shield against the effects of bad health habits, like smoking or not getting much exercise. But we know that you can't always eat like you should—and that sometimes you need more of a vitamin or mineral than you can reasonably get just from your food.

That's why vitamin and mineral supplements are so important. Taking a daily multivitamin and mineral supplement is sensible insurance—it makes sure you get everything you need. You may also need extra of one or more vitamins or minerals—more than you could get from your diet. Here, too, supplements make sure you're getting enough.

Generally speaking, vitamin and mineral supplements are safe even in large doses. More isn't always better, though, and some supplements can be harmful in big doses. Use your common sense. Read what we have to say about the vitamins and minerals, talk it over with your doctor, and then decide which supplements are best for you.

The Antioxidant Revolution

You need vitamins and minerals to make all those thousands of enzymes, hormones, and other chemicals your body needs to work right. But vitamins and minerals have another crucial role in your body: They act as powerful antioxidants that capture *free radicals* in your body. It's only in the past few decades that we've begun to understand how damaging free radicals can be and how important it is to have plenty of antioxidants in your body to neutralize them.

What's in a Word?

Free radicals are unstable oxygen atoms created by your body's natural processes and the effects of toxins such as cigarette smoke. Free radicals, especially singlet oxygen and hydroxyl, cause damage to your cells, but they're not all bad. You use free radicals as part of your immune system to defend against invading bacteria.

Radicals on the Loose

When you drive your car, you burn gasoline by combining it with oxygen in the pistons of the engine. Your car zips along on the released energy, but it also gives off exhaust fumes as a by-product. Something very similar happens in the cells of your body. When oxygen combines with glucose in your cells, for example, you make energy—and you also make free radicals, your body's version of exhaust fumes. Free radicals are oxygen atoms that are missing one electron from the pair the atom should have. When an atom is missing an electron from a pair, it becomes unstable and very reactive. That's because a free radical desperately wants to find another electron to fill in the gap, so it grabs an electron from the next atom it gets near. But when a free radical seizes an electron from another atom, the second atom then becomes a free radical, because now it's the one missing an electron. One free radical starts a cascade of new free radicals in your body. The free radicals blunder around, grabbing electrons from your cells—and doing a lot of damage to them at the same time.

Fighting Back with Antioxidants

Antioxidants are your body's natural defense against free radicals. *Antioxidants* are enzymes that patrol your cells looking for free radicals. When they find one, they grab hold of it and neutralize it without being damaged themselves. The antioxidant enzymes stop the invasion and remove the free radical from circulation.

What's in a Word?

Antioxidant enzymes protect your body by capturing free radicals and, in a complex series of steps, escorting them out of your body before they do any additional damage.

You have to have plenty of vitamins and minerals, especially vitamin A, beta carotene, vitamin C, vitamin E, and selenium, in your body to make the antioxidant enzymes that do the neutralizing. If you're short on the right vitamins and minerals, you can't make enough of the antioxidant enzymes. That lets the free radicals get the upper hand and do extra damage to your cells before they get quenched.

Oxidation isn't the only thing that can cause free radicals in your cells. The ultraviolet light in sunshine can do it—that's why people who spend too much time in the sun are more likely to get skin cancer and cataracts. Toxins of all sorts—tobacco smoke, the natural chemicals found in our food, the poisonous wastes of your own metabolism, and man-made toxins like air pollution and pesticides—trigger free radicals as well.

On average, every cell in your body comes under attack from a free radical once every 10 seconds. Your best protection is to keep your antioxidant levels high.

Understanding RDAs, or How Much Is Enough?

The nonprofit, independent Institute of Medicine (part of the National Academy of Science) is the organization that determines the RDAs, or Recommended Dietary Allowances. RDAs set the national guidelines for the minimum amounts you need to get every day. They're the basis for all the scientific research on nutrition—and for the information we give in this book.

You'll often encounter a related standard called the USRDA. This is the "other" RDA, set by the Food and Drug Administration, a federal agency. "US" stands for United States, of course, but this time "RDA" stands for Recommended Daily Allowance. The USRDAs are really just somewhat simplified versions of the Institute of Medicine's RDAs.

The RDA standard from the Institute of Medicine is slowly being phased out in favor of a new one called DRI, or Daily Reference Intake. For each vitamin and mineral, the DRI is sort of an average based on four measurements: the estimated average requirement; the RDA; the adequate intake; and the tolerable upper intake level. The new DRIs will gradually replace the old RDAs. Likewise, the USRDA standard will eventually be replaced by a new standard called the RDI, for Reference Daily Intake.

In the opinion of many health professionals, the amounts for vitamins and minerals are too low. More and more research tells us that larger doses of some vitamins and minerals not only keep you healthier now, they can also help diseases from getting started and can help control them once they do.

Vitamins and Minerals for Everyone

We feel almost everyone can benefit from vitamins and minerals beyond the RDAs. To help you decide how much more, we've created a very conservative table showing the safe ranges for healthy adults. Remember, more isn't always better. When in doubt, less is always best. Don't exceed the maximum safe dose!

Safe Dosage Ranges for Vitamins and Minerals for Healthy Adults

Vitamins	Safe Daily Dosage Range
Vitamin A	5,000–25,000 IU
B vitamins:	
Thiamin	2–100 mg
Riboflavin	50–100 mg
Niacin	20–100 mg
Pyridoxine	3–50 mg
Folic acid	800 mcg–2 mg
Cobalamin	500–1,000 mcg
Pantothenic acid	4–7 mg
Biotin	30–100 mcg
Vitamin C	500–2,000 mg
Vitamin D	400–600 IU
Vitamin E	200–400 IU
Calcium	1,000–1,500 mg
Copper 1.5–3.0 mg	
Chromium	50–200 mcg

Vitamins	Safe Daily Dosage Range
Iron	15–30 mg
Magnesium	300–500 mg
Manganese	2.5–5.0 mg
Molybdenum	75–250 mcg
Potassium	2,000–3,500 mg
Selenium	70–200 mcg
Zinc	15–50 mg

IU = International Units
mg = milligrams
mcg = micrograms

Whenever you visit any health-care professional, be sure to bring along a list of everything you take—including *all* prescription and nonprescription drugs and *all* vitamins, minerals, and other supplements. Otherwise, you might end up with an accidental bad reaction to a drug.

Taking Your Vitamins

Many people like the convenience of taking a one-a-day supplement—a pill you can pop first thing in the morning and not have to think about again. One-a-days have some drawbacks, though. First, many one-a-days just don't have enough in them. To keep them small enough to swallow easily, they don't have the RDAs for calcium, magnesium, or potassium. Most don't have the RDA for selenium, either. On the other hand, many one-a-day supplements do contain iron, which older adults should usually avoid. Another problem is that the water-soluble B vitamins and vitamin C will be washed from your body fairly quickly if you take them all at once.

Now You're Cooking

Store your vitamins in an opaque container or an amber glass bottle away from light, heat, and moisture. The bathroom isn't the best place for vitamins—there's too much moisture. A closed cupboard, closet, or drawer, well out of the reach of young children, is better.

It's much more effective to take your vitamins and minerals in divided doses throughout the day. That way, you can easily get the full RDAs for calcium and other minerals without having to swallow big pills, and your levels of the water-soluble vitamins remain high throughout the day. You'll get the most from your supplements if you make a habit of taking them with meals.

Check the freshness and potency guarantee date on supplements before you buy them. Pass on products that are near or past their expiration. To keep supplements fresh after you open them, buy only as much as you normally use in a month and put the lids back on tightly.

Chapter 2

Vitamin A and Carotenes: A+ Protection

In This Chapter

➤ Why you need vitamin A and carotenes

➤ Foods that are high in vitamin A and carotenes

➤ Choosing the right supplements

➤ How carotenes help protect you against the free radicals that can cause cancer and heart disease

When vitamin A was first discovered in 1913, it was called the "anti-infective agent." Lab animals fed a diet low in animal foods, vegetables, and fruits soon got eye infections—infections that cleared up as soon as these foods were put back into their diet. The mysterious "agent" in the foods turned out to be a fat-soluble substance that was dubbed vitamin A.

Why You Need Vitamin A

To fend off infections and illnesses, vitamin A helps you put up strong front-line barriers to infection. How? By helping your body's *epithelial tissues*—the cells that make up your skin and line your eyes, mouth, nose, throat, lungs, digestive tract, and urinary tract—grow and repair themselves. These tissues line your body's external and internal surfaces and keep out trespassers. Without enough vitamin A, these cells become stiff, dry, and much more likely to let their guard down. When that happens, germs can easily pass through them and into your body.

What's in a Word?

Your **epithelial tissues** cover the internal and external surfaces of your body. Since your skin covers all of your outside, it's one giant external epithelial tissue. Epithelial tissue also lines your nose and your eyes. Your entire digestive tract is lined with epithelial tissue. So are your lungs and your urinary and reproductive tracts.

Even if your body has plenty of vitamin A, those nasty germs still sometimes get through your outer defenses. When that happens, vitamin A helps your immune system come riding to the rescue.

Vitamin A is essential for healthy eyes—an important subject we'll talk a lot about later in this chapter.

Children and teens need plenty of vitamin A to help them grow properly and build strong bones and teeth. Your need for vitamin A doesn't stop then, though. Even after you're fully grown, your body constantly replaces old, worn-out cells with new ones. You need vitamin A to produce healthy replacement cells and to keep your bones and teeth strong.

Calling All Carotenes

Now that you know why you need vitamin A, we're going to confuse you by explaining why you need carotenes even more. Bear with us as we explain why.

When vitamin A was first discovered, researchers believed that the only way to get your A's was by eating animal foods such as eggs or liver that naturally contain *retinoids*, or *preformed vitamin A*. Your body can use this vitamin A as is just as soon as you eat it.

What's in a Word?

Vitamin A that comes directly from animal foods such as eggs is also known as **retinoids** or **preformed vitamin A**. **Carotenes** are natural pigments in red, orange, and yellow plant foods (cantaloupes, carrots, and tomatoes) and in potatoes and dark-green leafy vegetables. The name comes from carrots. Because your body has to change the carotenes into vitamin A before you can use them, carotenes are sometimes called **precursor vitamin A** or **provitamin A**.

In 1928, researchers discovered the other way to get your A's: by eating plant foods that contain *carotenes*—the orange, red, and yellow substances that give plant foods their colors. The most abundant of the carotenes in plant foods is *beta carotene*. Your body easily converts beta carotene to vitamin A in your small intestine, where special enzymes split one molecule of beta carotene in half to make two molecules of vitamin A.

If you don't happen to need any vitamin A just then, you don't convert the beta carotene. Instead, a lot of it circulates in your blood and enters into your cells; the rest gets stored in your fatty tissues. Whenever you need some extra A's, your liver quickly converts the stored beta carotene.

Carotenes are just one small group of plant substances in the much larger *carotenoid* family. In this chapter we'll focus on the two main carotenes that are converted to vitamin A: *alpha carotene* (sometimes written α-carotene) and *beta carotene* (sometimes written ß-carotene). (A few other carotenes have some vitamin A activity, but it's so minor we don't really need to discuss them.)

Why is it better to convert your A's from the carotenes in plant foods rather than getting them straight from animal foods or supplements? There are some very good reasons:

➤ The *antioxidant power* of carotenes. About 40 percent of the carotenes you eat are converted to vitamin A in your liver and small intestine as you need it. The rest act as powerful antioxidants.

➤ The *safety* of carotenes. Large doses of supplemental vitamin A can be toxic—and some people show overdose symptoms even at lower doses. Your body converts carotenes to vitamin A only as needed, however, so it's almost impossible to overdose.

➤ The *health benefits* of fruits and vegetables. Carotenes are found in almost every fruit and vegetable. Five servings a day will give you all the vitamin A you need, along with plenty of other vitamins, minerals, antioxidants, and fiber.

The RDA for Vitamin A

Check out the following table for the RDA for vitamin A. If you eat a typical diet, you'll get some of your vitamin A the preformed way as retinoids from milk, eggs, and meat. You'll get the rest in the form of carotenes (mostly beta) from the fruits and vegetables you eat.

The RDA for Vitamin A

Age	Vitamin A in RE	Vitamin A in IU
Infants		
0–1 year	375	1,875
Children		
1–3 years	400	2,000
4–6 years	500	2,500
7–10 years	700	3,500
Adults		
Men 11+ years	1,000	5,000
Women 11+ years	800	4,000
Pregnant women	800	4,000
Nursing women	1,300	6,500

IU = International Units
RE = Retinol Equivalent

The RDA table gives vitamin A in two different measurements. That's because for decades, the standard measurement unit for vitamin A was the International Unit (IU). After 1980, the measurement unit was changed to the Retinol Equivalent (RE), which gives a more accurate idea of how much vitamin A is really in a food or supplement. In scientific research, the RE is now the standard unit. Most vitamin manufacturers, though, still list the vitamin A and beta carotene content on the label in International Units. To convert from IUs to REs, divide by five (in other words, 4,000 IUs are equal to 800 REs).

Now You're Cooking

When you eat one large raw carrot, here's what you get:

Beta carotene: 8,100 IU	Phosphorus: 26 mg
Vitamin C: 6 mg	Potassium: 247 mg
Calcium: 27 mg	Sodium: 34 mg
Iron: 0.5 mg	Fiber: 1.5 g
Magnesium: 25 mg	

Vitamin A is an essential nutrient, so it's got an established RDA. Beta carotene, although it's certainly important, isn't considered essential, so it doesn't have an RDA. How can you decide how much to take? The U.S. Department of Agriculture and the National Cancer Institute suggest a daily dose of 6 mg, but many nutritionists feel this is too low. Some think you should take as much as 30 mg a day. A good compromise might be 15 mg a day—roughly the equivalent of 25,000 IU (5,000 RE) of vitamin A. That's about five times the RDA for vitamin A, but without the toxic side effects.

Vitamin A Cautions

Taking supplements that contain the RDA for vitamin A is generally safe for everyone, but use caution. Vitamin A in large doses can be toxic, causing a condition called *hypervitaminosis A*. Symptoms of A overload include blurred vision, bone pain, headaches, diarrhea, loss of appetite, skin scaling and peeling, and muscular weakness. Vitamin A toxicity doesn't usually occur until you've been taking really large doses (more than 25,000 IU daily) for a long time, but don't take any chances—stick to the RDA.

Babies and children can reach toxic vitamin A levels at much smaller doses. Most multivitamin supplements contain only the RDA, but some contain 10,000 IU (2,000 RE) or even more. Read labels carefully and talk to your doctor before giving vitamins to babies and children.

Be very careful about vitamin A supplements if you are or might become pregnant. Too much vitamin A (over 5,000 IU or 1,000 RE) can cause birth defects, especially if taken in the first seven weeks of pregnancy—when you might not even realize you're pregnant. Today many doctors suggest that women of childbearing age take beta carotene instead of vitamin A supplements. It's almost impossible to take too much beta carotene.

Eating Your A's

The RDA assumes that you'll be getting most of your vitamin A from animal sources such as eggs, liver, poultry, milk, cheese, and other dairy products. That's a pretty good assumption, because most people don't eat that many fruits and vegetables and don't get much beta carotene from their diet. Animal foods that are high in vitamin A, however, also tend to be high in calories and cholesterol.

Nutritionists today strongly recommend getting your A's the beta carotene way, through five daily servings of fresh fruits and vegetables. One medium carrot contains over 8,000 IU of beta carotene—with no toxic side effects, no fat, and only 35 calories. Plus, you'll be getting the antioxidant protection carotenes provide.

The old saying, "Have a lot of color on your plate," is the best advice for eating your carotenes. Remember, carotenes are the substances that give foods such as carrots, tomatoes, sweet potatoes, and apricots their vivid color. Actually, carotenes are found in practically all vegetables and fruits, including dark-green leafy vegetables such as spinach and broccoli. The carotenes are there—you just can't see the bright reddish colors because they're disguised by the green.

Now You're Cooking

Cooking destroys some of the carotenes in vegetables, but also releases others by breaking down tough cell membranes. On the whole, you absorb more carotenes from cooked veggies. Cook vegetables lightly in as little water as possible—steaming is a great way to preserve nutrients. Baking or grilling also gently releases the beta carotene.

Which Type Should I Take?

Vitamin A supplements usually come in soft gel caps in retinol or retinyl palmitate form—either is fine, but retinyl palmitate is best for people with intestinal problems. An old-fashioned way to get your A's is by taking cod liver oil. Aside from the fact that it's truly horrible tasting—even the cherry-flavored kind is awful—cod liver oil isn't a good choice. It's high in calories and often causes digestive upsets. Don't overdo on the vitamin A supplements— more than 5,000 IU (1,000 RE) a day can be harmful.

To avoid possible problems, we suggest taking mixed carotenes instead—you'll get your A's along with extra antioxidant protection. Look for a product that contains beta carotene along with at least 20 percent alpha carotene and also lutein, zeaxanthin, and lycopene.

Quack, Quack

Some manufacturers offer micellized or emulsified vitamin A—the vitamin A is broken up into tiny droplets—claiming this improves absorption. In fact, you absorb about 80 to 90 percent of plain old vitamin A. If you buy the micellized or emulsified brands, you'll be spending a lot more, but not absorbing much more.

Bugs Bunny Had Great Eyesight

Elmer Fudd never catches that pesky wabbit because Bugs always sees him coming. Why does Bugs have such great eyesight? It's all those carrots. What's good for Bugs is good for you, too. Vitamin A and beta carotene are essential for your eyesight. You need them to help prevent night blindness and prevent cataracts. You also need them to help prevent age-related macular degeneration (AMD), which is the leading cause of blindness in people over 65; about 30 percent of Americans over 75 suffer from it. According to one study, eating just one serving a day of a food high in beta carotene could reduce your chances of AMD by 40 percent.

A as in Aging Skin

The cells of your skin grow very rapidly—your outer skin turns over completely in just about four weeks. All rapidly growing cells, including those in your skin, need plenty of vitamin A. An early symptom of vitamin A deficiency is skin that is rough, dry, and scaly. To help keep your skin smooth and supple, make sure to get the RDA for vitamin A. This is especially important as you get older and your risk of skin cancer rises. One recent study shows that taking vitamin A could cut your chances of getting basal cell carcinoma, the most common type of skin cancer, by 70 percent.

To Beta or Not to Beta ...

... that is the cancer question. There's been a lot of controversy recently about beta carotene and cancer. Does it prevent cancer or not? Yes—or maybe not. Let's try and sort out the issues here.

Study after study shows that if you have a high beta carotene level because you eat a lot of foods that contain carotenoids, you're less likely to get cancer. In one important study, for example, 8,000 men were followed for five years. The ones who had the lowest intake of beta carotene had the highest risk of lung cancer. Almost all researchers today agree that beta carotene *foods* play a major role in preventing cancer, especially cancer of the lung, stomach, and cervix. The real question is, do beta carotene *supplements* prevent cancer? Some recent studies have shown that the supplements may not play much of a role. Beta carotene supplements alone can't overcome a lifetime of smoking, drinking, and eating a diet low in the valuable nutrients found in fruits and vegetables. Also, people who eat foods high in beta carotene are also eating lots of other carotenoids—and *you need a range of carotenoids, not just beta carotene, to help ward off cancer.*

WARNING: If you smoke, don't take beta carotene supplements! Studies prove that beta carotene supplements may have a bad effect on people who are already at high risk for lung cancer.

Carotenes and Cardiac Cases

As with cancer, so with heart disease. People who eat foods high in beta carotene definitely have fewer heart attacks and strokes. In one major study of women nurses, for example, the ones who ate the most beta carotene foods had 22 percent fewer heart attacks than those who ate the least. The biggest beta carotene eaters did even better when it came to strokes—they had 40 percent fewer.

Boosting Your Immunity with Vitamin A

The anti-infective powers of vitamin A have been known ever since the vitamin was discovered. For example, extra vitamin A is valuable for helping children get over the measles faster and with fewer complications. It also seems to help babies with respiratory infections. (Talk to your doctor before you give vitamin A supplements to babies or children.)

Chapter 3

B Healthy

In This Chapter

➤ Why you need the entire B family of vitamins

➤ How the B family protects your heart, gives you energy, boosts your immune system, and keeps you mentally alert

➤ What each B vitamin does for your health

➤ Foods that are high in B vitamins

The vitamins in the B family are all closely related. Here are the branches of the B family tree:

➤ **Thiamin, or vitamin B_1.** You need thiamin to keep all your body's cells, but especially your nerves, working right. Thiamin is important for mental functions, especially memory. You also need it to convert food to energy.

➤ **Riboflavin, or vitamin B_2.** Riboflavin is really important for releasing energy from food. It's also vital for normal growth and development, normal red blood cells, and for making many of your body's hormones.

➤ **Niacin, or vitamin B_3.** More than 50 body processes, from releasing energy from food to making hormones to detoxifying chemicals, depend on niacin.

➤ **Pantothenic acid, or vitamin B_5.** This vitamin works closely with several of the other B's in the breakdown of fats, proteins, and carbohydrates into energy. You also need it to make vitamin D, some hormones, and red blood cells.

➤ **Pyridoxine, or vitamin B_6.** The main job of pyridoxine is shuffling around your amino acids to make the 5,000+ proteins your body needs to run properly. It's also involved in making more than 60 different enzymes.

➤ **Biotin, or vitamin B_7.** Biotin is needed for a lot of body processes that break down fats, proteins, and carbohydrates into fuel you can use. Biotin is sometimes called vitamin H.

➤ **Folic acid, or vitamin B_9.** The main job for folic acid is helping your cells grow and divide properly—it's important for preventing birth defects. You also need it for making the natural chemicals that control your mood, your appetite, and how well you sleep. And folic acid is vital for keeping your arteries open and lowering your chances of a heart attack or stroke.

➤ **Cobalamin, or vitamin B_{12}.** You need cobalamin to process the carbohydrates, proteins, and fats in your food into energy. It also forms the protective covering of your nerve cells, keeps your red blood cells healthy, and helps prevent heart disease.

➤ **Choline.** This B vitamin works closely with folic acid and cobalamin to make neurotransmitters—chemical messengers that carry information to and from your brain. It's also crucial for making the membranes of your cells.

➤ **Inositol.** You need inositol to make healthy cell membranes and messenger chemicals. It's also sometimes helpful for relieving nerve damage from diabetes.

➤ **PABA.** The initials stand for para-aminobenzoic acid. This powerful antioxidant protects your skin from sun damage and is found in many sunscreen lotions and creams.

DRIs for B Vitamins

The DRIs for the B vitamins are a little controversial these days. That's because several of the RDAs (the old standard) were lowered in the 1989 recommendations. New DRIs (the new standard—check back to Chapter 1, "The A to K of Nutrition," for more information) for B vitamins were released in 1998. The amounts for folic acid were raised somewhat, to 400 mcg, and some of the other B recommendations were changed a little. Overall, however, the new DRIs are a disappointment to the many nutritionists and researchers who believe that higher amounts of all the B's, especially of folic acid, could do a lot to improve everyone's health. We'll discuss the DRIs further when we get to each B vitamin later in this chapter.

Here's one good reason many people think the DRIs for B vitamins should be higher. A major study in the prestigious *New England Journal of Medicine* in 1995 showed that people with high blood levels of a substance called homocysteine were much more likely to have clogged arteries, which means they were more likely to have a heart attack. Folic acid, pyridoxine, and cobalamin break down homocysteine. The higher your levels of these three B's, the lower your homocysteine level and the healthier your heart. How much healthier? The people with the highest B levels cut their risk of a heart attack *in half.*

Two thirds of the people with dangerously high homocysteine had inadequate levels of the three vital B's. Could there be a better example of how important vitamins are to your health?

Aging and the B Vitamins

Studies show that many elderly people are low in B vitamins, particularly cobalamin. Part of the reason is that you just don't absorb as many B's from your food as you grow older. Because some of the B's aren't absorbed all that well in the first place, older people can easily start to be deficient. Then the deficiency makes them a little depressed, so they eat less and get even fewer B's, which makes them more depressed or so forgetful that they eat even less, which makes them so forgetful, confused, and depressed that they end up in a nursing home. The food there might not help—institutional food often has most of its vitamins processed or cooked away.

Thinking About Thiamin

Your body goes through an amazingly complex series of steps to turn the food you eat into energy. All the B vitamins are involved in every one of those steps, alone or working together, but let's focus just on thiamin here. One particular step in the process needs an enzyme called *thiamin pyrophosphate*, or *TPP*, to work. Without thiamin, you can't make the enzyme—and without the enzyme, the whole process grinds to a halt.

What's in a Word?

Thiamin pyrophosphate (called **TPP** for short) is an enzyme your body needs to convert carbohydrates into energy. You need thiamin to make it—no other B vitamin can.

You need thiamin to keep your brain and nervous system fueled up. Thiamin helps keep your heart muscles elastic and working smoothly, which keeps your heart pumping strongly and evenly, with just the right number of beats.

The DRI for Thiamin

The amount of thiamin you need daily for good health is very small—the DRI for an adult male is only 1.2 mg. Check the following table to make sure you're getting your daily requirement.

The DRI for Thiamin

Age/Sex	Thiamin in mg
Infants	
0–0.5 year	0.2
0.5–1 year	0.3
Children	
1–3 years	0.5
4–8 years	0.6
9–13 years	0.9
Adults	
Men 14–18 years	1.2
Men 19–30 years	1.2
Men 31–50 years	1.2
Men 51+ years	1.2
Women 14–18 years	1.0
Women 19–30 years	1.1
Women 31+ years	1.1
Pregnant women	1.4
Nursing women	1.6

Thiamin Deficiency

You need so little thiamin, and it's so easily found in the typical diet, that few people are seriously deficient. There's one very big exception to that last statement: people who abuse alcohol. In fact, so many people in the developed world abuse alcohol that thiamin deficiency may be the most common vitamin deficiency of all.

Why does alcohol have such an impact on your thiamin level? There are several related reasons. Alcoholics tend to eat poorly, so their vitamin intake in general is very low. They don't eat enough thiamin, and the alcohol destroys most of what little they do take in. Alcohol also makes them excrete more thiamin. Chronic alcoholics need large amounts of thiamin supplements—anywhere from 10 to 100 mg day.

Eventually, thiamin deficiency from alcoholism causes a type of nerve damage called Wernicke-Korsakoff syndrome. The symptoms can usually be helped by giving up alcohol and eating a good diet, but the syndrome only worsens and leads to death if alcohol abuse continues.

Eating Your Thiamin

What do bagels and brown rice have in common? They're both good sources of thiamin. Actually, thiamin is found in lots of different foods; It's also added to flour, breads, pasta, and breakfast cereals. Because you need less than 2 mg to meet the DRI, most people get enough from their diet. Even someone who eats mostly burgers and fries will get enough thiamin, although just barely.

Wheat germ, sunflower seeds, whole grains, and all kinds of nuts are excellent food sources of thiamin. Beans and peas are also good sources. Some other good sources are oranges, raisins, asparagus, cauliflower, potatoes, milk, and whole-wheat bread. Oatmeal, whole wheat, and brown rice are grains that are high in thiamin. Among meats, pork and beef liver are high in thiamin; there's some in all beef and chicken.

Now You're Cooking

Meats preserve their thiamin best if they are cooked only until done—overcooking at high temperatures destroys thiamin. On the other hand, thiamin isn't affected by freezing.

B Energetic: Riboflavin

Riboflavin gives you energy at the most basic level—inside your cells. You need it to make two of the enzymes that are absolutely vital for releasing energy from the fats, carbohydrates, and proteins you eat. To make a complicated story short, riboflavin keeps you alive.

Aside from that little chore, riboflavin also does a bunch of other things in your body, either by itself or along with the other members of the B team (especially pyridoxine and niacin). Riboflavin regulates cell growth and reproduction and helps you make healthy red blood cells. It helps your immune system by keeping the mucous membranes that line your respiratory and digestive systems in good shape. If invading germs still sneak in, riboflavin helps you make antibodies for fighting them off. Your eyes, nerves, skin, nails, and hair all need riboflavin to stay healthy. It might even help your memory—older people with high levels of riboflavin do better on memory tests.

The DRI for Riboflavin

Important as riboflavin is, you don't really need a lot of it for good health—well under 2 mg a day is enough. Check the following table to see how much you need per day.

The DRI for Riboflavin

Age/Sex	Riboflavin in mg
Infants	
0–0.5 year	0.3
0.5–1 year	0.4
Children	
1–3 years	0.5
4–8 years	0.6
9–13 years	0.9
Adults	
Men 14–18 years	1.3
Men 19–30 years	1.3
Men 31+ years	1.3
Women 14–18 years	1.0
Women 19–30 years	1.1
Women 31+ years	1.1
Pregnant women	1.4
Nursing women	1.8

Eating Your Riboflavin

Large amounts of riboflavin are found in milk and other dairy foods. Good choices here include cheese, yogurt, and ice cream. Meat, especially liver, is a good source of riboflavin, as is fish. Vegetable foods that are high in riboflavin include broccoli, spinach, avocados, mushrooms, and asparagus. Most breads, baked goods, and pasta are made with flour that has been enriched with riboflavin and other B vitamins; most breakfast cereals also have riboflavin and other B's added to them.

Now You're Cooking

Riboflavin does not break down in cooking. Avoid adding baking soda to vegetables, though. It helps the veggies keep their color, but it destroys the riboflavin.

Preventing Migraines with Riboflavin

There's no headache quite so awful as a migraine. There's the terrible pain along with nausea, vomiting, and sensitivity to light. Because these headaches are so incapacitating, and because they affect some 11 to 18 million Americans every year, a lot of research goes into them.

One of the more interesting recent studies showed that high daily doses of riboflavin—400 mg a day—sharply reduced the number and severity of migraine attacks for over half the participants. The researchers think it works because people who get migraines have low cellular energy reserves in their brains. Riboflavin helps the cells use energy better, which seems to help prevent the migraines to begin with and make them less severe when they do happen. And unlike many other drugs used to treat migraines, riboflavin is cheap, safe, and has no side effects. The research is still in the early stages, however, so if you want to try high doses of riboflavin for your migraines, talk to your doctor first.

Niacin Is Nice

Niacin is essential for more than 50 different processes in your body. What most of these processes boil down to is helping your body produce energy from the foods you eat. Niacin makes enzymes that help your cells turn carbohydrates into energy. As part of the energy end of things, niacin also helps control how much glucose (sugar) is in your blood, which in turn helps give you energy when you need it—when you exercise, for example.

The DRI for Niacin

The DRI for niacin is based mostly on how many calories you eat—but which foods those calories come from is also part of the picture. The calorie part is easy: At a bare minimum, you need about 7 mg of niacin for every 1,000 calories you eat. This ratio assumes that you eat 2,000 calories a day and get at least 14 to 16 mg of niacin a day. If you don't eat that much (say, you're dieting), you still need the same amount of niacin.

Here's where the food part comes in. You probably think your niacin comes straight from your food. Well, most of it does, but some is also made in your body from the proteins you eat. It works like this: When you eat animal or plant protein, your body breaks the proteins down into their building blocks—amino acids. One of those building blocks is the amino acid *tryptophan*.

Your body uses about half your tryptophan for making some of the 50,000+ proteins you need. The other half gets converted to niacin. In fact, only about half your niacin comes directly from the foods you eat; the other half is converted from tryptophan. You need about 60 mg of tryptophan to make 1 mg of niacin. Because most people eat somewhere between 500 to 1,000 mg of tryptophan a day, they make about 8 to 17 mg of niacin.

What's in a Word?

Tryptophan is one of the nine essential amino acids—you can only get it from your food. Your body uses half the tryptophan it gets to help make the thousands of complicated proteins that keep you running. The rest is converted to niacin. The best way to get your tryptophan is through the proteins in your food.

The DRI chart ignores tryptophan and only counts the niacin you get as preformed niacin from your food. That's why, even though studies show that most Americans get only about 11 mg of niacin from their diet, very few people are actually deficient—they make up the rest of the DRI from tryptophan. To be on the safe side, though, try to get your full DRI from foods rich in niacin.

The DRI for Niacin

Age/Sex	Niacin in mg
Infants	
0–0.5 year	2.0
0.5–1 year	3.0
Children	
1–3 years	6.0
4–8 years	8.0
9–13 years	12.0

continues

The DRI for Niacin (continued)

Age/Sex	Niacin in mg
Adults	
Men 14–18 years	16.0
Men 19–30 years	16.0
Men 31–50 years	16.0
Men 51+ years	15.0
Women 14–18 years	14.0
Women 19–30 years	14.0
Women 31+ years	14.0
Pregnant women	18.0
Nursing women	20.0

Eating Your Niacin

Niacin is found in lots of common foods, especially meat, fish, poultry, eggs, and whole grains. It's also added to breakfast cereals, rice, bread, and many baked goods. Tryptophan is found in just about every protein food, especially milk, dairy foods, and eggs. Most people can easily get their DRI for niacin and tryptophan from their diet. Strict vegetarians and vegans need to eat plenty of nuts and whole grains such as oatmeal to meet their DRIs. Remember that about half of the tryptophan you consume is converted into niacin. The rest of this amino acid is used to help make the proteins that keep you going.

Pellagra—the deficiency disease caused by a lack of niacin—was a widespread problem throughout the South until well into the twentieth century. Some 200,000 people were affected every year. For a long time, doctors thought a germ of some sort caused pellagra. It was only in the 1920s that a dedicated public health physician, Dr. Joseph Goldberger, showed that a poor diet was the cause.

Now You're Cooking

Native Americans ate a lot of corn, low in both niacin and tryptophan, but never got pellagra. They soaked dried corn kernels in water mixed with wood ashes. The mixture made it easy to slip off the tough outer skin, made the corn easier to digest, and also made the niacin and tryptophan easier to absorb.

Cholesterol B Gone

You can't open a newspaper or magazine today without seeing big ads that trumpet drugs to treat high cholesterol. The ads tell you how well the drugs work and how they even help prevent heart attacks. If you look more closely at those ads, though, you'll see paragraph after paragraph of tiny type describing the side effects in scary detail.

The one thing that's not mentioned in the ads is the cost. These drugs are expensive. A month's supply of pravastatin (Pravachol®) costs about $70—and you'll probably be taking it for the rest of your life.

For some people, there's a better and cheaper way: niacin. Doctors have known for many years that large doses of nicotinic acid—between 2 and 3 g a day—lower LDL ("bad") cholesterol and triglycerides and raise HDL ("good") cholesterol. Lowering your LDL cholesterol and triglycerides, and raising your HDL cholesterol, definitely decreases your risk of a heart attack. In fact, a major study that went on for 15 years showed not only that the group who took niacin had lower cholesterol and fewer heart attacks, they also had fewer deaths for any reason.

WARNING: *Do not try niacin supplements on your own to lower your cholesterol.* The doses needed are so high that the niacin stops being a supplement and becomes a drug. You must work with your doctor and have your cholesterol and liver functions checked often. If you are already taking a cholesterol drug, don't stop taking it and switch to niacin. Also, don't keep taking your cholesterol drug and start taking niacin as well. Discuss your cholesterol and the drugs you take with your doctor before trying niacin.

Not everyone with high cholesterol should take niacin. If you have diabetes, extra niacin could cause your blood sugar to go up. If you have gout, extra niacin could trigger an attack. If you take medicine for high blood pressure, niacin could make your blood pressure drop too low. And if you have liver disease or ulcers, niacin could make these problems worse.

Boy, Was My Face Red

Large (and even not-so-large) doses of nicotinic acid cause a nasty side effect called the niacin flush. About 15 to 30 minutes after you take it, your face and neck get really red and hot—you blush so badly it reminds you of being back in junior high. The flush can go on for half an hour or longer and then wears off.

The best way to avoid flushing may be to avoid nicotinic acid and take niacin in the form of *inositol hexaniacinate* (*IHN*). Doctors in Europe have been prescribing IHN for more than 30 years, but it's only recently become available in the United States. IHN works on cholesterol just as well as nicotinic acid, but without the side effects. If you'd like to try IHN, talk to your doctor.

Pyridoxine with a Purpose

You need pyridoxine (also known as vitamin B_6) to turn the proteins you eat into the proteins your body needs, and you need it to convert carbohydrates from the form you store them in into the form you can use for energy.

What sort of proteins does your body need? For starters, hemoglobin—the stuff that carries oxygen in your red blood cells. Pyridoxine is needed to make lots of other proteins including hormones, neurotransmitters, and enzymes. You also need it to make prostaglandins, hormone-like substances that regulate things like your blood pressure.

The DRI for Pyridoxine
You don't need a lot of pyridoxine for basic good health. Just under 2 mg a day is plenty for an adult. Check the following table to see what the DRI is.

The DRI for Pyridoxine

Age/Sex	Pyridoxine in mg
Infants	
0–0.5 year	0.1
0.5–1 year	0.3
Children	
1–3 years	0.5
4–8 years	0.6
9–13 years	1.0
Adults	
Men 14–18 years	1.3
Men 19–50 years	1.3
Men 51+ years	1.7
Women 14–18 years	1.2
Women 19–50 years	1.3
Women 51+ years	1.5
Pregnant women	1.9
Nursing women	2.1

Eating Your Pyridoxine

The best source of pyridoxine in your food is high-quality protein: chicken, pork, beef, fish, milk, dairy products, and eggs. Milk, dairy products, and eggs have less pyridoxine than fish and other meats, but they're still good sources. Also, pyridoxine is added to flour, corn meal, breakfast cereals, and many baked goods.

Here's a rare case where we can't tell you to eat more fresh fruits and vegetables: Most of them don't have much or any pyridoxine. Even broccoli, our old standby, has only 0.15 mg in a half cup. The best plant choices are avocados, bananas, mangos, and potatoes. Whole grains are also good.

Be very, very cautious about taking pyridoxine supplements. This is one of the few water-soluble supplements that you can actually overdose on. Too much pyridoxine causes neurological problems such as numbness or tingling in the hands and feet and trouble walking. The symptoms usually go away if you cut back on the dose, but sometimes they're permanent. Talk to your doctor.

Help for Heart Disease

Folic acid combines with pyridoxine and cobalamin to fight heart disease by breaking down homocysteine. You need all three working together for the maximum effect.

On its own, pyridoxine plays some other roles that also help prevent heart disease. One of the most important is keeping your red blood cells from getting "sticky" and clumping together, or aggregating. When that happens, the cells release powerful chemicals that eventually cause atherosclerosis—deposits that clog up your arteries and could lead to a heart attack or stroke.

If enough cells clump together, they form a clot that blocks an artery. Again, the result is a heart attack or stroke. If you're at risk for atherosclerosis or already have it, taking pyridoxine supplements could slow the process down. Talk to your doctor before you try it, however.

Now You're Cooking

Fruits and vegetables don't contain all that much pyridoxine. The best choice in fruit is bananas—one medium banana has 0.66 mg. Among the vegetables, potatoes are a good choice. One baked potato with the skin has 0.70 mg. If you skip the skin, the potato has only 0.47 mg.

Pyridoxine supplements in fairly high doses—about 500 mg a day—can lower your blood pressure. It's cheaper than prescription drugs and doesn't have their side effects, but you do have to worry about the possible side effects of the large dose. Don't try this on your own, especially if you already take medicine to lower your blood pressure. If you want to try pyridoxine, talk to your doctor first.

Helping Asthmatics

Some people with asthma benefit from pyridoxine supplements, possibly because their bodies don't use it properly to begin with. Taking extra may bring their pyridoxine level closer to normal, which reduces their wheezing and cuts back on how often they have attacks.

A drug called theophylline is widely prescribed for asthma—and also for bronchitis and emphysema. It's an effective treatment, but it has a lot of bad side effects, including headaches, nausea, irritability, tremors, sleeping problems, and even seizures. The side effects are caused because theophylline blocks the way your body uses pyridoxine. Even if you're taking in enough through your food, the drug is keeping you from using it. Pyridoxine supplements have been shown to reduce the side effects of theophylline, especially tremors. If you're taking this drug, talk to your doctor about pyridoxine supplements before you try them.

Relief for Carpal Tunnel Syndrome

Your wrist is a marvel of engineering. To make this joint flexible, bones, ligaments, and muscles all come tightly together, leaving only a narrow passage—the carpal tunnel—for the nerves leading to your hand. If anything swells up in your wrist, even a little, it presses on the passage and squeezes the nerves. The result? *Carpal tunnel syndrome (CTS)*, a painful problem that is becoming very common. Symptoms include pain, numbness, and tingling in the fingers, wrist, or hand. Women seem to get CTS more often than men.

Quack, Quack

Some manufacturers offer pyridoxine supplements in the form of P-5-P (pyridoxal-5-phosphate) tablets. They claim this form is more active and more absorbable. Unless you have liver disease (in which case your doctor will probably suggest P-5-P shots), stick to plain old pyridoxine. It works just as well and costs a lot less.

A lot of people claim that pyridoxine supplements help or even "cure" CTS. Is there any evidence for this? Not really. Careful studies show that hardly anyone with CTS is deficient or even low in pyridoxine. The studies also show no real benefit from treating CTS just with large doses of pyridoxine—and as we discussed earlier, large doses could be

dangerous. It's possible that pyridoxine can help, however, if it's taken in moderate doses (150 mg a day) along
with other treatments, such as physical therapy and drugs
to relieve the swelling.

Pyridoxine for PMS

Researchers have been looking into pyridoxine for treating
PMS ever since the early 1970s. There have been more
than a dozen serious studies, and none of them have
proved that pyridoxine does much one way or the other.
In the studies, women who took pyridoxine felt that their
symptoms, including depression, irritability, headaches,
and fluid retention, got better. The problem is that the
women who thought they were taking pyridoxine, but
were actually taking sugar pills, also felt their symptoms
got better.

So should you take pyridoxine for PMS? Studies aside,
many of Dr. Pressman's patients really have benefited
from this, so we suggest you try taking 50 mg a day in the
days before your period. It won't hurt, and there's a good
chance it might help.

Folic Acid: Healthy Babies, Healthy Hearts

You need folic acid (also called folate) for the normal
growth and maintenance of every cell in your body. Folic
acid does some other amazing things for your health. In
the past few years we've learned that folic acid prevents
birth defects, helps prevent heart disease, and may even
help prevent cancer.

The DRI for Folic Acid

In 1989, the RDA for folic acid was lowered by about half.
The earlier RDA for adult males, for example, was 400
mcg; this was reduced to 200 mcg. The RDA for women of
childbearing age was also cut in half, from 800 mcg to 400

mcg. Studies in the 1980s showed that although the average folic acid intake for all age groups was considerably below the RDA, few people showed any sign of deficiency. So, the reasoning went, the RDA should be lowered to the amount taken in on average by most healthy people, because they all seemed to be okay.

In 1998, the Institute of Medicine looked at the evidence and raised the new DRI for folic acid up to 400 mcg for all adults and 600 mcg for pregnant women. The DRIs for children were also raised. Many doctors and nutritionists believe that the adult DRI is still way, way too low. They feel every adult should get at least 400 mcg of folic acid every day, but 800 mcg would be even better.

The DRI for Folic Acid

Age/Sex	Folic Acid in mcg
Infants	
0–0.5 year	65
0.5–1 year	80
Children	
1–3 years	150
4–8 years	200
9–13 years	300
Adults	
Men 14+ years	400
Women 14+ years	400
Pregnant women	600
Nursing women	500

Are You Deficient?

Even after the RDA for folic acid was lowered, studies show that the average American diet contains only about 200 mcg a day. Not surprisingly, a shortage of folic acid by the new higher DRI is one of the most common vitamin deficiencies, especially among women. One recent study estimated that an astonishing 88 percent of all Americans get less than 400 mcg a day.

Eating Your Folic Acid

Popeye the Sailorman always eats his spinach so he'll be strong to the finish. Why does Popeye eat spinach instead of one of those other dark-green leafy vegetables we keep talking about, like collard greens, or maybe Swiss chard? Aside from the fact that those vegetables don't rhyme with finish, they don't have anywhere near as much folic acid.

Now You're Cooking

Beans are an excellent natural source of folic acid—but there is that embarrassing little problem. Beans produce gas. To reduce the problem, soak dried beans in nine cups of water for every cup of beans. Change the water at least twice during the 24-hour soaking period. Drain and rinse before using.

Folic acid isn't found in that many animal foods. The only good animal sources are chicken liver and beef liver; there's hardly any in milk and other dairy foods. Beans of all kinds are a great way to get your folic acid; so is wheat germ. Other good plant sources are spinach and asparagus. On the whole, most fruits don't contain much folic acid. The best choices are bananas, oranges, and cantaloupe.

Because most Americans don't begin to eat enough beans and fresh vegetables, the FDA has prepared new rules for fortifying enriched breads, flours, corn meal, rice, noodles, pasta, and other grain products with folic acid. As of 1998 all these foods have extra folic acid added to them. The goal is to make sure that everyone gets at least 400 mcg a day from their food.

Folic Acid for Healthy Babies

Every year in the United States about 2,500 babies are born with a *neural tube defect* (NTD). About one to two out of every 1,000 births—11 a day—in the United States have a neural tube defect. The most common is the crippling defect spina bifida, or "open spine." Recent studies have conclusively shown that taking 400 mcg of folic acid each day *before* getting pregnant can prevent between 50 and 75 percent of all neural tube defects. In 1992, the U.S. Public Health Service recommended that *all* women of childbearing age consume 400 mcg of folic acid daily. Every agency and organization concerned with birth defects, from the FDA to the March of Dimes, has strongly endorsed this recommendation.

What's in a Word?

A **neural tube defect (NTD)** happens when the growing brain, spinal cord, and vertebrae (the bones of the spine) of an unborn baby don't develop properly during the first month of pregnancy.

Why does everyone recommend folic acid for all women, not just women who are pregnant? Your unborn baby needs folic acid the most during the first month of pregnancy, when the neural tube is formed—but you might not realize you're pregnant during that critical time, even if you've been trying to have a baby. It's vitally important for every woman to get enough folic acid. If you're a woman between the ages of 15 and 47, the time to start taking folic acid supplements is *now*.

Folic Acid Forestalls Heart Disease

Remember our discussion of the dangers of artery-damaging homocysteine earlier in this chapter? Keeping your homocysteine level low is one of the jobs of folic acid. Working with pyridoxine and cobalamin, folic acid quickly breaks down the homocysteine and removes it from your body before it can do any damage.

Now here's the really big question: How much folic acid is enough to keep your homocysteine level low? Only 1 to 2 mg a day—not very much, but a lot more than the DRI.

Getting more folic acid, through your diet or with supplements, is simple, safe, and cheap—and it could save your life. By some estimates, just 1 mg a day could be enough to prevent 50,000 heart attacks a year.

Preventing Cancer with Folic Acid

For a long time, cancer researchers were so focused on the powerful antioxidant vitamins A, C, and E that they sort of forgot about the B vitamins. Recently, though, folic acid has been getting a lot of attention for its role in preventing cancer. If you're a woman and get a lot of folic acid in your diet, your chances of colon cancer are sharply lower—by as much as 60 percent. (For some reason, this doesn't work as well for men.) Folic acid may also help prevent cancer of the cervix.

Cobalamin for Your Cells

Cobalamin, also known as vitamin B_{12}, does plenty for you, but let's start with its most important role: making healthy red blood cells. If you eat enough cobalamin, and if your body can use it properly, you make millions of nice, round, healthy red blood cells every day. If you don't eat enough, or you can't use it properly, you can't make enough red blood cells, and the ones you do make are too large and fragile to work well. When you don't have enough red blood cells to carry oxygen and nutrients around your body, you develop anemia.

All your cells, not just your red blood cells, need cobalamin to grow and divide properly. For example, you need it to make all the different cells in your immune system, including white blood cells.

Cobalamin's next big role is in making the protective fatty layer, or sheath, that lines your nerve cells—sort of like insulation on electric wires. If the sheath is damaged because you don't have enough cobalamin, you start getting the equivalent of static on the line. Really bad static can interfere with your mental function—so much that people think you're senile.

Cobalamin is also a team player. Working with the other B vitamins, but especially with pyridoxine and folic acid, it helps you turn the carbs, fats, and proteins in your food into energy in your cells, and helps remove harmful homocysteine from your blood before it can damage your blood vessels.

The DRI for Cobalamin

Important as cobalamin is, you need only very small amounts of it. That's why the DRI for an adult is only 2.4 mcg. The DRI doesn't take into account the fact that you absorb less cobalamin as you get older. Many doctors and nutritionists now feel that people over age 50 need a lot more cobalamin. Doctors usually recommend daily supplements containing 500 to 1,000 mcg. It's a safe and inexpensive form of health insurance. At the least, check the DRI table to be sure you're getting the minimum.

The DRI for Cobalamin

Age	Cobalamin in mcg
Infants	
0–0.5 year	0.4
0.5–1 year	0.5
Children	
1–3 years	0.9
4–8 years	1.2
9–13 years	1.8
Adults	
14+ years	2.4
Pregnant women	2.6
Nursing women	2.6

Are You Deficient in Cobalamin?

That's an important question, because it can be hard to tell. To understand why, we'll have to explain how cobalamin gets into your body. Cobalamin is found only in animal foods such as liver, eggs, fish, and meat—and only in very small amounts that are hard to take in. To get even the small amount of cobalamin you need, your body needs to be really good at absorbing it. In fact, you make a special substance in your stomach, called *intrinsic factor*, just to help you do that—and even that only lets you absorb about half of the cobalamin you eat. Fortunately, most people take in more than twice the DRI through their diet, so they usually get enough.

What's in a Word?

To absorb cobalamin from your food, your stomach naturally secretes a special substance called **intrinsic factor**. Without it, you can't absorb the cobalamin.

If you don't get much cobalamin in your diet, it could take a long time—four or five years—for deficiency symptoms to start showing up. Sometimes people slowly stop making intrinsic factor, but here, too, it could take several years for real deficiency symptoms to appear.

WARNING: *Large doses of vitamin C can destroy cobalamin; take these supplement an hour or more apart, not at the same time.*

The most obvious symptom of cobalamin deficiency is anemia—in this case, because you don't have enough healthy red blood cells. When the anemia comes from a shortage of cobalamin in the diet, it's called *megaloblastic anemia*. When it comes from a lack of intrinsic factor, it's called *pernicious anemia*. The causes are different, but the result is the same: You don't have enough red blood cells, and the ones you do have are too big and fragile to survive long in your circulation.

On the whole, most people under age 50 get enough cobalamin from their diet, but older people and strict vegetarians and vegans are at real risk for a deficiency.

Eating Your Cobalamin

Only animal foods such as meat, fish, and eggs naturally have cobalamin in them (it's added to some breakfast cereals). Even then they don't have much—but on the other hand, you don't need much, so most people get enough from their diet.

Now You're Cooking

People who don't eat animal foods often rely on soybean foods for their cobalamin. However, many soy products contain very little cobalamin, even when the labels say otherwise. Plant foods such as spirulina, sea vegetable, and brewer's yeast don't have cobalamin in a form your body can use. To be safe, take cobalamin supplements.

The big exceptions are people who are strict vegetarians, vegans, or follow a macrobiotic diet. Because they eat no meat and sometimes no animal foods at all, they have to get their cobalamin from some other source. In the diet, that source is usually soybean foods, but these probably don't provide enough, especially for children. If you don't eat meat or animal foods, we strongly suggest you take cobalamin supplements.

The Other B Vitamins

The other members of the B family—biotin, choline, inositol, PABA, and pantothenic acid—are all important to your overall health, but there just isn't all that much to say about them. Pantothenic acid is found in just about every food you eat, so it's impossible to be deficient in it. Ditto for choline. Friendly bacteria in your intestines make all the biotin you need and some of your inositol (you get the rest from food). PABA is made in your body from folic acid.

Most of the claims made for these B vitamins don't have much basis, so there's practically never any need to take them in supplements or even think about them.

Chapter 4

Vitamin C: First Choice

In This Chapter

➤ Why you need vitamin C

➤ Foods that are high in vitamin C

➤ Choosing the right supplement for you

➤ How vitamin C can help prevent heart disease and cancer

➤ How vitamin C can help other health problems such as the common cold

Half of all American adults take extra vitamin C. Can 50 million people be wrong? Not in this case, anyway. Those people know that a daily dose of vitamin C helps keep them healthy—and they also know that when they're sick, vitamin C can help them feel better faster. It may even help them live longer. A recent study shows that men who take vitamin C supplements live, on average, six years longer than those who don't.

Why You Need Vitamin C

There's not much vitamin C *doesn't* do for you. You need it for more than 300 different purposes in your body. Just for starters, vitamin C is needed to make *collagen,* the strong connective tissue that holds your skeleton together, attaches your muscles to your bones, builds strong blood vessels, and keeps your organs and skin in place. Collagen is the glue that holds your body together—and you can't make it unless you have enough vitamin C. (The next time someone tells you to pull yourself together, maybe you should reach for the C supplements!)

What's in a Word?

The connective tissue that holds your cells together and makes up your bones, tendons, muscles, teeth, skin, blood vessels, and every other part of you is made from a protein called **collagen.**

Because you need collagen to fix damage to your body, it stands to reason that vitamin C helps heal wounds of all sorts. Broken bones, sprained joints, cuts, and other injuries all heal a lot faster if your body gets plenty of vitamin C.

Vitamin C is your body's top antioxidant. Not only does it mop up those nasty free radicals, it helps many of your body's other antioxidants do their work better. And without vitamin C, you can't use some other vitamins and minerals, like folic acid and iron, properly.

Your immune system needs a lot of vitamin C to run at peak levels. If you don't get enough, you're likely to get sick more often and to stay sick longer. You also need vitamin C to manufacture many of your body's hormones.

Vitamin C also does things, like curing some types of male infertility and helping diabetics, that make it seem more like a miracle drug than a plain old vitamin. People with high levels of vitamin C have lower blood pressure, which makes them less likely to have a stroke or heart attack. And although vitamin C can't cure heart disease or cancer, it could help keep you from getting them in the first place.

What about the common cold? Not even vitamin C prevents or cures that. If you do catch a cold, though, vitamin C may help you feel better sooner.

The RDA for Vitamin C

Humans, unlike almost all other animals, can't manufacture vitamin C in their bodies. Because vitamin C is water-soluble, you also can't store it in your body for very long. Both these facts mean that you need to have a new supply on a regular daily basis through the foods you eat and the supplements you take.

As you'll see from the following table, the adult RDA for vitamin C is only 60 mg—an amount many researchers now believe is too low. The Institute of Medicine, the organization that sets the RDAs, is now discussing raising the minimum for vitamin C to somewhere between 100 and 200 mg daily. Vitamin C is found in so many common fruits and vegetables that almost everyone in our modern society gets about 100 mg a day without even trying.

The RDA for Vitamin C

Age/Sex	Vitamin C in mg
Infants	
0–0.5 year	30
0.5–1 year	35

continues

The RDA for Vitamin C   (continued)

Age/Sex	Vitamin C in mg
Children	
1–3 years	40
4–6 years	45
7–10 years	50
11–14 years	50
Adults	
Men 15+ years	60
Women 15+ years	60
Pregnant women	70
Nursing women	95

The RDAs in the table are for people who don't smoke.
Smokers have below-normal levels of vitamin C—as much
as 40 percent lower in pack-a-day smokers. Cigarettes rob
your body of vitamin C by breaking it down and excreting
it much faster than normal. The Institute of Medicine recommends 100 mg a day for smokers and is considering
raising this to 200 mg. We think this number is way too
low. If you smoke, consider taking 1,000 mg daily. This
amount could also help protect you against two types of
cancer smokers often get: cancer of the larynx and cancer
of the esophagus.

Eating Your C's

You know from all those OJ ads that oranges and other
citrus fruits are a great way to get your C's. But did you
know that there's as much vitamin C in one kiwi as there
is in an orange (about 80 mg)? Or that a tangerine has less
than half the vitamin C of an orange? There's some vitamin C in just about every fruit and green vegetable. Strawberries, melons, and cranberries are high in vitamin C.

Tropical fruits such as guavas, mangos, and papayas are all high in vitamin C—as high as oranges or higher.

Dark-green leafy vegetables such as spinach and kale are fairly good sources of vitamin C. Vegetables such as broccoli, Brussels sprouts, peppers, potatoes, turnips, and tomatoes are also good dietary sources.

Now You're Cooking

To help preserve the vitamin C in foods, buy the freshest fruits and vegetables you can, store them in a cool, dark place, and use them as soon as possible. A lot of vitamin C is lost when foods are cooked. Try to cook vegetables very lightly in as little water as possible.

There's some, though not a lot, of vitamin C in meat, poultry, fish, milk, and dairy products. Beans generally have little or no vitamin C, and there's none in grains such as oats or wheat.

Freezing preserves most of the vitamin C in vegetables and fruits. Canned vegetables are cooked and then packed in water, which pretty much destroys the vitamin C. Canned fruits have almost no vitamin C, but they do have a lot of added sugar. Go for the fresh fruits whenever you can.

Getting the Most from Vitamin C

Because vitamin C is water-soluble, it's almost impossible to overdose or reach toxic levels even when you take large doses—the excess passes harmlessly out in your urine. The usual safety range is from 500 to 4,000 mg a day. Large doses sometimes cause stomach upsets, diarrhea, and cramping, however. The problem usually starts at doses over 2,000 mg, but children and some adults are more sensitive. If you want to take large amounts of vitamin C, start with smaller doses and gradually build up until you get diarrhea. Cut back until the problem goes away and then stick with that dose. Nutritionists call this "reaching bowel tolerance."

Take your total vitamin C dose in several small doses spread throughout the day. Each dose is gone from your body within four hours, so spreading them out helps keep your level steady. We suggest taking your supplements with each meal and before bed.

If you've ever had a kidney stone or if you have kidney disease, your doctor will probably advise against taking large doses of vitamin C. Doses up to a 1,000 mg a day or even more are unlikely to cause kidney stones, but if you have kidney problems, discuss vitamin C supplements with your doctor before trying them.

Which Type Should I Take?

The vitamin C shelves have got to be the most confusing place in any health-food store. Do you want to take your C's in capsules, tablets, or chewable tablets? Or do you prefer powder, crystals, or liquid, or maybe chewing gum or syrup? Read on—it's not as complicated as it seems.

Quack, Quack

The makers of esterized vitamin C (or Ester-C ascorbate) say it is absorbed faster, used better, and excreted slower. It also costs more than plain ascorbic acid. Save your money. There's no major difference.

Vitamin C is ascorbic acid and ascorbic acid is vitamin C, whether it's synthesized in a lab or extracted "naturally" from rose hips. In fact, most of the vitamin C sold today is made from corn, and it's all pretty much the same. Stick to a reliable, inexpensive brand, and don't waste your money on the stuff that claims it's better because it's "organic" or "natural."

Vitamin C breaks down when it is exposed to light, heat, water, or air. Buy just a few weeks' worth at a time from a store that turns over its stock quickly. Store your C's in a cool, dark, dry place.

Front–Line Antioxidant

It's this simple: *Vitamin C is the most important antioxidant in your body.* You need vitamin C as your front-line defense against free radicals (remember those destructive molecules from Chapter 1, "The A to K of Nutrition"?). Job one for vitamin C is to capture free radicals and neutralize them before they can do any damage to your cells.

Dealing with free radicals is the main job of lots of other vitamins and minerals in your body. What makes vitamin C so important? First, because it's water-soluble, it's everywhere in your body—inside all your cells and in the spaces in between. Because free radicals are also everywhere, vitamin C is always on the spot to track them down. Second, and just as important, other powerful antioxidants such as vitamin E and antioxidant enzymes such as superoxide dismutase (SOD) and glutathione need vitamin C to work properly.

Preventing Cardiovascular Disease

According to some pretty careful studies of data from the National Center for Health Statistics, if every adult in the United States took an extra 500 mg of vitamin C a day, about 100,000 of them wouldn't die of heart disease every year. Not only would all those people still be alive and kicking, they wouldn't be costing *billions* of dollars in health-care expenses every year. Here's where vitamin C pays dividends in both better health and in real dollars and cents. A year's supply of vitamin C costs under $45; a coronary bypass operation costs about $45,000.

Vitamin C helps your heart in two main ways. First, studies show that people with high levels of vitamin C have lower total cholesterol levels. Second, numerous studies show that people with high levels of vitamin C have blood pressure readings that are slightly lower than people with low C levels.

Curing the Common Cold

Does vitamin C keep you from catching a cold, flu, bronchitis, or pneumonia? No. Does it help you get better faster if you do? Yes. If you're basically healthy and take 1,000 to 2,000 mg of extra vitamin C, your cold symptoms will probably be less severe and you'll get better a little faster. Vitamin C works against colds and other illnesses because all the different kinds of immune cells and the complex chemical messengers that tell them what to do all need plenty of C's to work at peak efficiency.

Healing Wounds

One sign of scurvy—the deficiency disease caused by a lack of vitamin C—is wounds that won't heal or old wounds that reopen. That's because you need vitamin C to make collagen, which is what makes scar tissue and heals wounds. Extra vitamin C will help you heal faster if you have a cut, scrape, broken bone, burn, or any other sort of wound.

Diabetes and Vitamin C

Diabetics, especially those with non-insulin-dependent, adult-onset (Type II or NIDDM) diabetes, often have low vitamin C levels. If you have diabetes, your doctor will probably recommend that you take 500 or 1,000 mg a day of extra vitamin C. Some diabetics say that their circulatory problems and other complications get a lot better when they take larger doses, as high as 3,000 mg a day or even more. They also say that they can control their blood sugar better when they take large doses. It's also possible that extra vitamin C could help prevent diabetic cataracts. Talk to your doctor before you start taking large doses of vitamin C for diabetes.

Cancer and Vitamin C

Before we go any further into vitamin C and cancer, let's clear up a few things. Yes, vitamin C can definitely help prevent cancer. No, vitamin C does not cure cancer. Maybe, vitamin C helps treat cancer. Let's take these one at a time.

Preventing Cancer

Study after study after study proves that vitamin C can help protect you against cancer. People with high levels of vitamin C and other antioxidants are markedly less likely to get cancer of the lung, cervix, colon, pancreas, esophagus, mouth, and stomach. Why? We're still not sure, but it's very likely that the antioxidants gobble up free radicals and damaging toxins before they can damage your cells and trigger cancer. In the case of stomach cancer, vitamin C blocks the formation of cancer-causing nitrosamines from the nitrates and nitrites found in bacon, hot dogs, and other cured meats.

Curing Cancer

A study by Dr. Linus Pauling in 1976 showed that some terminally ill cancer patients lived as much as a year longer if they took megadoses (over 10,000 mg) of vitamin C. A later study backed this up. In both studies, though, all the patients eventually died—none was cured.

No study since then has ever shown that megadoses of vitamin C (or any other vitamin, for that matter) cure cancer.

Quack, Quack

There is no evidence that megadoses of vitamin C cure cancer. Sadly, some unscrupulous people claim otherwise, promising to "cure" your cancer with expensive vitamins and other weird supplements and treatments. Your health and even your life are at stake—don't fall for this sort of quackery.

Treating Cancer

If you're being treated for cancer, there's no question that vitamin C can really help you get through this difficult time. Many people getting radiation treatment or chemotherapy have low vitamin C levels. Part of the reason is that the treatment can make you tired and nauseous, as well as giving you diarrhea. The other part is that the treatment makes you produce huge amounts of free radicals, so any vitamin C you get from your food mops them up. Unless you take supplements, you won't have any left over for other things, like keeping your immune system active. Cancer treatment lowers your immunity, making you more likely to get sick or pick up an infection.

Discuss nutrition and supplements, especially vitamin C, with your doctor *before* you start your cancer treatment. They could make a big difference in how well you do.

C-ing Is Believing

Vitamin C can help prevent cataracts—clouding of the lens in your eye that can lead to blindness—as you grow older. A 1997 study by researchers at Tufts University and Harvard University School of Medicine found that taking vitamin C supplements over a long period—10 years or more—lowered the risk of cataracts among older women by an amazing 77 percent. Even women who had other risk factors for cataracts, such as smoking, were protected if they took vitamin C supplements. The researchers believe the antioxidant powers of vitamin C are the key here. The extra C's mop up free radicals in your eyes before they can damage the delicate lens. How much vitamin C do you need for eye protection? The study suggests 250 mg a day does the trick.

Vitamin D: Soak It Up

Vitamin D's most important role is to regulate how much calcium you absorb from your food. Most of that calcium goes to build strong bones and teeth. You also need calcium to send messages along your nerves and to help your muscles contract (like when your heart beats). Vitamin D regulates the amount of calcium in your blood and makes sure you always have enough. We're just starting to realize that vitamin D also plays a role in a lot of other body functions. Your immune system needs vitamin D, and it may help prevent cancer, especially colon cancer.

The Sunshine Vitamin

Vitamin D is the eccentric uncle of the vitamin family—it does things its own way. To get all the other vitamins, you have to eat them. To get vitamin D, all you have to do is go outside. That's because you actually make vitamin D when the sun shines on your skin. Even eccentric uncles act normal sometimes, though—and so does vitamin D. It's found naturally in a few foods, but in a slightly different form called vitamin D_2, or *ergocalciferol*. Your body can use this just as well—in fact, it's the form that's used in most vitamin D supplements.

What's in a Word?

The vitamin D you get from foods or supplements is called vitamin D_2 or **ergocalciferol**. The *ergo-* comes from ergot, a fungus that grows on rye plants. Substances in ergot cause hallucinations—LSD was first made from ergot. Although vitamin D was discovered in ergot, your daily supplement is made from yeast or fish liver and can't cause hallucinations.

The RDA for Vitamin D

For years, many researchers said the RDA was too low for older people. You just naturally make less vitamin D in your skin as you get older—which is one of the reasons older people tend to have fragile bones. In 1997, the recommended amounts for vitamin D were changed to account for age changes. The Institute of Medicine decided not to set an RDA or DRI, though. Instead, the vitamin D amounts are now called Adequate Intakes (AIs) and are based on the amounts needed "to sustain a defined nutritional status." In other words, the AI is the amount you need to maintain a basic level of good health.

Although the AI is given in micrograms (mcg), the vitamin D in food and supplements is generally measured in

International Units (IUs). One microgram equals 40 IU. We use both measurements in the following AI table for vitamin D.

Adequate Intakes for Vitamin D

Age/Sex	Vitamin D in mcg	Vitamin D in IU
Infants, Children, and Adolescents		
0–18 years	5	200
Adults		
19–50 years	5	200
51–70 years	10	400
71+ years	15	600
Pregnant women	5	200
Nursing women	5	200

Many nutritionists and doctors feel that you need even more vitamin D as you get older to keep your bones strong and avoid osteoporosis—a disease that makes your bones thin, brittle, and easily broken. An important study published in *The New England Journal of Medicine* in 1997 backs them up. The study showed that men and women over age 65 can cut their risk of a bone fracture in half if they take 700 IU of vitamin D and 500 mg of calcium every day. (We'll talk more about osteoporosis in Chapter 8, "Calcium: Boning Up!")

Eating Your D's

Long before anyone knew what caused rickets (vitamin D wasn't discovered until the 1930s), they knew that choking down a daily spoonful of awful-tasting cod-liver oil prevented it. Fish oil contains a lot of vitamin D, so you get some from eating fish liver, mackerel, herring, sardines, salmon, tuna, and other oily fish.

What's in a Word?

Fortified milk has vitamin D and (sometimes) vitamin A added. In the 1930s milk producers began adding 400 IU to every quart in an effort to eliminate rickets, caused by a crippling shortage of vitamin D. Without it, bones can't absorb enough calcium to grow straight and strong.

There aren't that many other foods that naturally have vitamin D. Beef liver, egg yolks, butter, and margarine all have some, though not a lot. Plant foods have almost none, but vitamin D is added to a lot of breakfast cereals. Today almost all the vitamin D people get from their diet comes from *fortified milk*. There isn't naturally much vitamin D in milk, but milk producers have been adding 400 IU of it to every quart of milk—whole, skim, low-fat, and nonfat—for decades. It's the reason rickets has practically disappeared. There's no vitamin D in most milk products, though. Cheese, yogurt, cottage cheese, and other dairy foods aren't made with fortified milk, so they don't have much or any vitamin D. Also, raw milk, most organic milk, and goat's milk don't have added vitamin D. Margarine, however, is fortified with vitamin D.

Getting the Most from Vitamin D

If you spend a lot of time outdoors in the sun, your body automatically stops making vitamin D after you've stored up enough. In other words, you can't overdose on sunshine.

Now You're Cooking

You'll absorb your D's a lot better if you take them with some dietary fat. Take your D supplements with a meal.

The same definitely isn't true of vitamin D supplements. Of all the vitamins, this is the one you need to be most careful with. Large doses can make calcium build up in your blood, which could have serious consequences—although this is very unlikely in doses under 1,000 IU. Too much vitamin D might also increase your risk of a heart attack or kidney stones.

On the other hand, most people get only about 50 to 70 IU in their diet, so if you're not outside much, supplements might be a good idea—especially in the winter. And as we mentioned earlier, if you're an older adult you might need vitamin D supplements.

Most multivitamin supplements have 200 IU, which meets the AI for people under 50 even if you never get any sun or drink any milk. If you decide to take additional supplements, be on the safe side and keep your total daily dose to no more than 1,000 IU. Talk to your pediatrician before giving vitamin D supplements to babies and children.

Vitamin D and Cancer

We've known for a long time that colon cancer and breast cancer are more common among people in northern climates—places where it's too cold for part of the year to get much sun. Is there a vitamin D connection?

Quack, Quack

A lot of worthless claims are made for vitamin D. There's no evidence that it cures or even helps acne, arthritis, herpes, or cystic fibrosis. It also doesn't "cure" alcoholism. Don't be taken in, and remember, large doses of vitamin D can be dangerous.

Yes, when it comes to colon cancer—and maybe also breast and prostate cancer. According to recent studies, people who get a lot of vitamin D from their food and supplements are much less likely to get colon cancer. To get the protection, you only need to get 200 IU from your diet—the amount in just 2 cups of milk. Do you get the same protection if you just stay outside in the sun longer? Probably, but it's really hard to say exactly how much vitamin D you make from sunshine. To be sure you're getting enough, take supplements.

Vitamin D not only helps prevent cancer, it can help treat it. The powerful anticancer drug tamoxifen, which is widely used to treat cancer of the ovaries, uterus, and breast, seems to work even better when it's combined with small doses of vitamin D. It's also possible that vitamin D can help treat leukemia and lymphoma, but there's not enough research yet to be sure.

Other Health Problems Helped by Vitamin D

Vitamin D can help strengthen your immune system in general. In particular, you need it to make monocytes, special white blood cells that fight off infections. About

5 percent of your white blood cells are monocytes, so a shortage of vitamin D could leave you wide open to infection.

Helping Psoriasis

Psoriasis is a chronic skin disease that makes your skin get itchy red flaky patches. Sunshine seems to help clear up the patches for some people. Likewise, a prescription skin cream that has vitamin D in it seems to help. Just taking a lot of vitamin D in supplements doesn't though—and it could be dangerous. If you have psoriasis, talk to your doctor about vitamin D creams.

Helping Your Hearing

Many adults lose some of their hearing as they grow older. In fact, more than one out of every four adults over age 65 has some hearing loss. In some cases, a shortage of vitamin D may have damaged the delicate ear bones—and it's possible that taking vitamin D supplements can help restore some hearing. This doesn't work in every case, of course, so talk to your doctor before you try it.

Chapter 6

Vitamin E: Excalibur!

In This Chapter

➤ Why you need vitamin E

➤ How vitamin E prevents heart disease

➤ Boosting your immunity with vitamin E

➤ How vitamin E helps prevent cancer

➤ Why you need extra vitamin E as you get older

You need vitamin E for one big reason: free radicals. We know, we know—we're always talking about these dangerous little vandals. What makes vitamin E so special? Vitamin E is special because it's especially good at protecting your cell membranes against free radicals—and damage to your cell membranes is often the first step down a slippery slope that can lead to cancer, heart disease, and other health problems.

Vitamin E works so well as an antioxidant because it's a fat-soluble vitamin—and your cell membranes are made up mostly of fat. Vitamin E gets into the membrane and lassos any free radicals that try to get through.

Vitamin E also teams up with vitamin A, beta carotene, and vitamin C, the other major antioxidant vitamins, to give you extra protection.

In the past few years, a number of important studies on the benefits of vitamin E supplements have been in prestigious medical publications like the *Journal of the American Medical Association*. Mainstream medicine is catching on to something nutritionists have known for a long time: Vitamin E really does help prevent heart disease—and if you already have heart disease, vitamin E can help keep it from getting worse. The studies also show that vitamin E can help prevent cancer and strokes, boost your immunity, and help problems such as diabetes. Best of all, vitamin E supplements, even in large doses, are very safe.

The RDA for Vitamin E

It's hard to figure out an exact RDA for vitamin E. That's because how much you need depends in part on your body size: The heavier you are, the more you need. It also depends in part on how much fat you get in your diet from plant foods and fish. Here, too, the more fat you eat, the more vitamin E you need.

What's in a Word?

In 1922, researchers found that lab rats on a diet of highly processed foods with no fats couldn't have babies. When the rats were given wheat-germ oil—high in vitamin E—they became fertile again. Vitamin E was originally called **tocopherol,** from the Greek words *tokos,* meaning "offspring," and *pheros,* meaning "to bear."

The RDA is based on natural alpha *tocopherol,* because that's the most active form of vitamin E. Nutritionists often count the vitamin E in food in milligrams (mg), because foods contain mixed tocopherols. Scientific types like to count the vitamin E in terms of International Units (IUs) of alpha tocopherol, because that's the most common and active form. One milligram of vitamin E is equal to 1.49 IU. The RDA is shown both ways in the following table.

The RDA for Vitamin E

Age/Sex	Vitamin E in mg	Vitamin E in IU
Infants		
0–1 year	3–4	4.5–6.0
Children		
1–10 years	6–7	9.0–10.5
Young Adults and Adults		
Men 11+ years	10	15
Women 11+ years	8	12
Pregnant women	10	1512
Nursing women	12	18

Along with many other nutritionists and doctors, we're going to ignore the RDA and suggest much higher doses—100 IU or even more—in the rest of this chapter. Fortunately, doses this large and even much larger are safe.

Eating Your E's

There just aren't that many foods that contain vitamin E. The only ones that really have any are vegetable oils, seeds, wheat germ, and nuts. The best food source is wheat-germ oil—1 tablespoon has 20 mg. An ounce of roasted sunflower seeds has 14 mg, but an ounce of dry-roasted almonds has just under 7 mg. There's a little vitamin E in plant foods such as avocados (2.32 mg per half), asparagus (less than 1 mg in four cooked spears), mangos (just over 2 mg in a whole one), and sweet potatoes (nearly 6 mg in a medium one), but it's hardly worth mentioning. Animal foods such as meat and milk have practically no vitamin E.

Now You're Cooking

A lot of the vitamin E in vegetable oils is lost in processing. To get the most E's from a vegetable oil, buy cold-pressed, unbleached safflower oil. You'll probably have to get it at the health-food store.

The benefits of vitamin E really kick in only at daily amounts over 100 IU. There's no way you can eat that much vitamin E—in fact, it's hard to eat even 25 IU. To get 100 IU from food, you'd have to eat about 15 ounces of almonds (which would have over 2,500 calories) or swallow 5 tablespoons of wheat-germ oil (600 calories) or 22 tablespoons of safflower oil (over 2,600 calories). Supplements are the way to go.

WARNING: *If you take the blood-thinning drugs warfarin (Coumadin®) or heparin—or any other drug to thin your blood or prevent clots—do not take vitamin E supplements!* The combination could lead to dangerous bleeding. Talk to your doctor about all supplements before you try them.

What About Selenium?

The trace mineral selenium helps vitamin E work better and longer in your body. (We'll talk more about selenium in Chapter 12, "The Trace Minerals: A Little Goes a Long Way.") You need only very tiny amounts of it—the amount in your daily multivitamin/mineral supplement is usually plenty. If you think you're not getting enough selenium, though, try one of the vitamin E supplements that has added selenium.

E-vading Heart Disease

In the past few years, three really important studies have shown that people who take vitamin E supplements have less heart disease. One of the studies, the Cambridge Heart Antioxidant Study (CHAOS), looked at 40,000 men who already had heart disease and found that vitamin E kept their heart disease from getting worse. In fact, the men who took at least 400 IU of vitamin E cut their chances of a nonfatal heart attack by an amazing 77 percent. Another study looked at a group of over 87,000 women nurses and found that those who took vitamin E cut their overall risk of heart disease by about two thirds. Finally, a long-term study of over 34,000 postmenopausal women showed that those who ate the most foods high in vitamin E had strikingly less heart disease, even though they didn't take vitamin E supplements.

The explanation for this excellent news about evading heart disease? Vitamin E helps prevent *atherosclerosis* (hardening of the arteries) caused by *atheromas* or *plaque* on the walls of the arteries that lead to your heart. And how does vitamin E prevent this? By its powerful antioxidant action, which helps keep cholesterol in your blood from oxidizing into those artery-clogging deposits in the first place—and helps keep the deposits you may already have from getting worse.

What's in a Word?

Atherosclerosis is the medical term for hardening of the arteries. Atherosclerosis starts with fatty deposits called **atheromas** in your arteries. The atheroma slowly gets bigger and harder and turns into a waxy substance called **plaque.** The plaque narrows or even blocks the artery.

Vitamin E works because it is a powerful antioxidant that keeps your LDL ("bad") cholesterol from being oxidized. Less oxidized cholesterol, less plaque, less heart disease.

There's another way vitamin E helps prevent heart disease. If your arteries are narrow and clogged, tiny blood cells called platelets are likely to get stuck in the plaque. Red blood cells then get stuck in the platelets and form a blood clot. If the clot gets big enough, it blocks the artery and causes a heart attack. Vitamin E helps keep the platelets from sticking, so clots don't form as easily.

The same anti-clotting effect of vitamin E also helps protect you from having a stroke—a blood clot or blockage in an artery leading to your brain. In 1999, an important study showed that people who take just 30 to 50 IU of extra vitamin E—the amount in a typical one-a-day vitamin—cut their risk of stroke by a whopping 53 percent.

Is It Really That E-Z?

Amazingly, a lot of doctors still aren't convinced about the benefits of vitamin E—they want more studies. They also point out that giving up smoking, drinking less alcohol, getting exercise, and eating better all help prevent heart disease. The docs have a good point: Your lifestyle counts. Vitamin E isn't a miracle drug or an excuse to keep smoking. Even so, the patients in the CHAOS study took either 400 or 800 IU of vitamin E a day. They didn't have any problems from the large doses, and their hearts were helped—even when they didn't change any unhealthy habits. The recent stroke study just underscores how valuable vitamin E can be.

WARNING: Very large doses of vitamin E (thousands of IU) can block your body's use of vitamin A.

E-luding Cancer

The evidence that vitamin E helps prevent cancer isn't as dramatic as for heart disease, but it's still pretty strong. Researchers have known for many years that people with cancer have low vitamin E levels. But do they have cancer because they have low vitamin E? Maybe, said the skeptics, they have low vitamin E because they have cancer.

We now know that people with low vitamin E levels are more likely to get cancer—in other words, low vitamin E could be a cause, not an effect. We also now know that people with high vitamin E levels are less likely to get cancer. Vitamin E's antioxidant effect seems to provide the protection. It mops up free radicals before they can do the sort of cell damage that leads to cancer.

Now You're Cooking

Vitamin E is broken down by high heat, light, and freezing temperatures. Store your vitamin E supplements in a cool, dark place, but don't let them freeze.

Here's a good example. A recent study at the National Cancer Institute looked at oral and throat cancer. People who took vitamin E supplements cut their chances of getting these types of cancer in half. Another good example: In a 1997 study, men who had the highest intake of vitamin E had the least chance of getting one common type of colon cancer. The protection was especially good for men over 60, who are at higher risk anyway. Their risk was cut an amazing 80 percent compared to the men who had the lowest intake. Here's a surprise, though: Vitamin E didn't do that much to protect women against colon cancer. Why? We don't know yet.

Vitamin E may also help protect against cancer of the cervix and breast cancer. We're a little less sure about lung cancer. Extra E probably helps protect you, but only if you don't smoke.

Excellent for the Elderly

As you get older—past 60 or so—your immune system naturally slows down. That makes you more likely to get sick with something serious that you can't fight off, like pneumonia or cancer.

There's recently been some excellent news for older adults about vitamin E and immunity—and it comes from the prestigious *Journal of the American Medical Association*. In a 1997 article, researchers showed that taking vitamin E can give your immune system a real boost. Healthy volunteers, all over age 65, took vitamin E supplements for 33 weeks. Tests at the end of that time showed that their immune systems were much more active. The best results came from taking 200 mg a day; taking more didn't seem to help more.

The news about Alzheimer's disease and vitamin E is good but not quite excellent. Vitamin E in large doses (2,000 IU) seems to slow down—although not stop or prevent—Alzheimer's. In fact, it works just as well as a more expensive prescription drug. The antioxidant power of vitamin E is probably what helps, because it seems to slow the breakdown of brain cells. This is a promising area of research for a devastating disease—we'll be watching it carefully.

If you're over age 60, it's probably time to start taking those extra E's—but talk to your doctor first, especially if you have any chronic health problems.

Chapter 7

Vitamin K: The Band-Aid in Your Blood

In This Chapter

➤ Why you need vitamin K

➤ Foods that are high in vitamin K

➤ How vitamin K helps your blood clot

➤ How vitamin K helps keep your bones strong

Vitamin K is essential for making the blood clots that quickly stop the bleeding whenever you injure yourself, but it has some other jobs as well. The most important is the role it plays in building your bones. Vitamin K is needed to help you hold onto the calcium in your bones and make sure it's getting to the right place. There's also some interesting research on vitamin K and cancer.

The RDA for Vitamin K

There's only been an RDA for vitamin K since 1989. Up until then, researchers thought that all the vitamin K you need was made for you by friendly bacteria in your intestines. In fact, though, the bacteria make only half or less of what you need. You get the rest mostly from—you guessed it—green leafy vegetables.

Now You're Cooking

The best food source of vitamin K is seaweed. There's about 1,500 mcg in 3 ounces of dried dulse or rockweed. Seagrass has about 200 mcg in 3 ounces and kelp (sea lettuce) only has about 60 mcg. Check for seaweed in your health-food store.

The amount of vitamin K in the RDA is based on your body weight. It's set at 1 mcg for every kilo (2.2 pounds) you weigh, so the numbers in the following table are for a mythical average person. If you're heavier than average, you might need more. If you're lighter than average, though, you should still get the RDA.

The RDA for Vitamin K

Age/Sex	Vitamin K in mcg
Infants	
0–0.5 year	5
0.5–1 year	10
Children	
1–3 years	15
4–6 years	20
7–10 years	30

Age/Sex	Vitamin K in mcg
Young Adults and Adults	
Men 11–14 years	45
Men 15–18 years	65
Men 19–24 years	70
Men 25+ years	80
Women 11–14 years	45
Women 15–18 years	55
Women 19–24 years	60
Women 25+ years	65
Pregnant women	65
Nursing women	65

Eating Your K's

A lot of foods haven't ever been analyzed to find out how much vitamin K they have. And in the ones that have been studied, the K amounts are variable—some sources give amounts that are a lot different than others. In general, though, all the dark-green leafy vegetables, like kale, broccoli, and cabbage, are good choices. Strawberries are also good. Some animal foods, including egg yolks and liver, have small amounts of vitamin K. Very little vitamin K is lost in cooking.

Most people get well over the RDA for vitamin K from their food and don't ever need to take a supplement. Not too many multivitamins have even small amounts of vitamin K in them, although you can buy K supplements in 100 mcg capsules. In fact, because supplements should be used only if your doctor has diagnosed a real vitamin K deficiency, you need a prescription for them in some states. If you want to make sure you're getting enough vitamin K, the best approach is to eat your vegetables.

Now You're Cooking

There are 199 mcg of vitamin K in 1 ounce of green tea leaves—but not in any other kind of tea. That sounds like a lot, until you realize that it takes a dozen tea bags to make 1 ounce. In other words, 1 cup of green tea has only about 16 mcg of vitamin K.

Vitamin K and Clotting

Your blood normally has a number of different *clotting factors*—substances that help it form clots to stop bleeding from cuts, bruises, and other injuries. You need vitamin K to help your liver make *prothrombin* (factor II), the most important of the clotting factors. Some of the other factors, including factors VII, IX, and X, are also made in your liver and also depend on vitamin K. Without clotting factors, your blood clots very slowly or not at all, so even a small cut can bleed for a long time and even a minor bang can cause a big bruise.

What's in a Word?

Clotting factors are substances in your blood that help it clot and stop bleeding. You make a lot of different clotting factors, but the most important is **prothrombin.** You need vitamin K to make prothrombin and several other clotting factors.

Vitamin K and Osteoporosis

You need vitamin K to help your bones grab onto calcium, put it in the right place, and hold onto it once it's there. If you don't have enough K, you won't be able to form new bone very well. In the long run, a shortage of vitamin K can lead to the disease called osteoporosis, or bones that are brittle and break easily. (We'll talk a lot more about osteoporosis in Chapter 8, "Calcium: Boning Up!")

Quack, Quack

Skin creams containing vitamin K and other "healing compounds" are said to make spider veins on your face and legs "disappear." The cost for these worthless creams? At least $15 an ounce. Save your money.

Once osteoporosis starts, researchers think that extra vitamin K may help slow down the process. This is still being studied, though, so don't start taking supplements just yet.

K Kills Cancer Cells

But so far, only in the test tube. Vitamin K seems to slow down or kill tumor cells in the lab just as well as powerful drugs. Some studies are looking at combining vitamin K with standard anticancer drugs to help them work better. The research continues—stay tuned for interesting developments.

Chapter 8

Calcium: Boning Up!

In This Chapter

➤ Why everyone needs calcium—and why women need extra

➤ How calcium keeps your bones strong all your life

➤ Foods that are high in calcium

➤ Choosing the right calcium supplement

➤ How calcium may help your blood pressure

Calcium is by far the most abundant mineral in your body. It makes up about 2 percent of your total body weight, or between 2 and 3 pounds if you're an average adult. Most of your calcium—98 percent of it—is in your bones. Another 1 percent is in your teeth, and the last 1 percent circulates in your blood. Small as the amount of calcium in your blood is, it's very important—so important that your body will pull calcium from your bones to make sure there's enough in your blood. Among other things, calcium helps regulate your heartbeat, control your blood pressure, clot your blood, contract your muscles, and send messages along your nerves. Calcium is needed to make many different hormones and enzymes, especially the ones that control your digestion and how you make energy and use fats. It also helps build your connective tissue and may help prevent high blood pressure and colon cancer.

Boning Up on Calcium

How many bones are in your skeleton? Give up? You have 206. Every single one of them is made up mostly of calcium phosphate, a very hard, dense mixture made when calcium and phosphorus combine.

Your bones may be hard, but they're also living tissue. You're constantly breaking down old bone and building new bone. From the time you're born until you get to be about 30 to 35 years old, you build up bone faster than you lose it, so your bones get bigger and denser, and you reach what's called peak bone mass. You could think of it as building up a bone savings account. After about age 35, you start to slowly break down bone faster than you can rebuild it—you start to draw on your saved-up bone. Some slow bone loss is a normal part of getting older, but if you don't get enough calcium, the process can start to happen too fast, especially in older women who've reached menopause. If you lose too much bone, you empty out your bone savings account. At that point, your bones are thin, brittle, and break very easily. Like some 25 million Americans—four out of five of them older women—you've got *osteoporosis*.

Here's where calcium comes in. If your bones are strong to begin with, and if you keep giving them plenty of calcium as you get older, you'll help keep your bones strong throughout your life. And even if osteoporosis has already set in, calcium may help slow it down.

What's in a Word?

Osteoporosis means bones that break easily because they are thin, porous, and brittle. The disease has several related causes, but too little calcium in the diet plays a big part in causing it.

The DRI for Calcium

In 1997, the Institute of Medicine raised the standard for calcium with the first of the new Dietary Reference Intakes (DRIs) that will gradually replace the old RDAs (check back to Chapter 1, "The A to K of Nutrition," for a more detailed explanation). Here's the new and improved DRI for calcium:

The DRI for Calcium

Age/Sex	Calcium in mg
Infants	
0–0.5 year	210
0.5–1 year	270
Children	
1–3 years	500
4–8 years	800
9–18 years	1,300

continues

The DRI for Calcium   (continued)

Age/Sex	Calcium in mg
Adults	
19–30 years	1,000
31–50 years	1,000
51+ years	1,200
Pregnant Women	
14–18 years	1,300
19–30 years	1,000
31–50 years	1,000
Nursing Women	
14–18 years	1,300
19–30 years	1,000
31–50 years	1,000

Over half of all young people today don't meet the DRI for calcium. That means they're not getting the calcium they need during the crucial childhood, teen, and young adult years to build up their bone mass. If you don't get enough calcium during these critical years, you don't build up your bone savings account, which could lead to big trouble when you're older.

It's not just kids who don't get enough calcium. Most women in the United States eat under 600 mg of calcium a day. In fact, calcium is the one nutrient most likely to be missing in the typical American diet. According to U.S. Department of Agriculture surveys, 90 percent of adult women aren't getting even 800 mg of calcium! The numbers aren't much better for teen-aged girls: 85 percent of them get only between 300 and 800 mg a day. Men do better, but even so, only 4 out of every 10 men is getting enough calcium. It's no wonder that today we have a virtual epidemic of osteoporosis—and that it's costing some $14 billion a year to treat all those broken bones. We'll have even more cases in the future as the population gets older. By one estimate, the number of hip fractures in the United States may triple by the year 2040.

Now You're Cooking

All milk—regular, skim, low-fat, 1 percent, 2 percent, nonfat—has the same amount of calcium: about 300 mg in 8 ounces. It's the same for all other dairy foods: low-fat and regular have the same amount of calcium.

Calcium-Robbing Drugs

Some common prescription and over-the-counter drugs can rob your body of calcium and lead to osteoporosis. If you regularly take any of these drugs, talk to your doctor about calcium supplements:

➤ Cortisone and other steroid drugs such as hydrocortisone, prednisone, and dexamethasone

➤ Thyroid supplements

➤ Cholestyramine (Cholybar® or Questran®), a drug used to treat high cholesterol

➤ Aluminum antacids

In addition, heavy drinkers and people who smoke have a higher risk for osteoporosis. If you do both, you're at even greater risk. Smokers have lower bone density than non-smokers (we don't really know why). In fact, a recent study showed that smoking doubles your risk of a hip fracture, even if you don't have osteoporosis. Alcohol interferes with your absorption of calcium. Also, heavy drinkers often don't eat very well and don't get enough calcium in their food. People under the influence tend to fall—and combined with osteoporosis this leads to broken bones.

Eating Your Calcium

Lots of favorite foods are rich in calcium—and a lot of common foods, including orange juice, are now available with added calcium. Milk and dairy products are by far the best sources of calcium. There's about 300 mg of calcium in one 8-ounce glass of milk. (Milk also has vitamin D, which you need to absorb calcium better and also to build your bones.) Yogurt usually has even more calcium than milk, and many yogurt makers are now adding extra calcium. The amounts vary from brand to brand, though, so read the labels carefully. An ounce of cheddar cheese has 200 mg, while an ounce of mozzarella has 147 mg, and a cup of low-fat cottage cheese has 138 mg.

Here's the best news of all: Ice cream is a good source of calcium. There's 85 mg in half a cup of plain vanilla ice cream. So next time you order a double-scoop cone, forget the calories and think of the calcium!

Now You're Cooking

Great news for caffeine addicts! For a long time, researchers thought caffeine made bone loss worse. The most recent study proves, however, that caffeine has nothing to do with bone loss.

Other good dietary sources of calcium are dark-green leafy vegetables, including broccoli, kale, and spinach. Beans, nuts, tofu (bean curd), and fish with soft, tiny bones (canned sardines and salmon are good choices) also give you plenty of calcium.

Picking the Right Calcium Supplement

Let's face it: The only way a lot of us are going to get enough calcium each day is to take supplements. But just look at how many different supplements are on the shelf at the store. How can you pick the right one for you from all those choices? Supplements made with calcium carbonate are the least expensive, but they dissolve slowly in your stomach, so you may not get the benefit of all the calcium. Along with many doctors and nutritionists, we recommend supplements made with calcium citrate or calcium lactate—your body can absorb the calcium from these supplements easily.

WARNING: You don't have to wait for a fracture to tell if your bones are thinning. One early warning sign is trouble with your teeth. If your dentures stop fitting right, it might be because of bone loss in your jaw. If you're at risk for osteoporosis, talk to your doctor about having a bone density test. New X-ray techniques make this quick, safe, and easy.

Calcium Supplements to Avoid

Adding to all the calcium confusion are three forms you should not take, no matter how large the word "natural" is on the label:

➤ **Bone meal.** A powder made from the ground bones of cattle, bone meal has over 1,500 mg of calcium in a 5-gram serving, along with other minerals such as phosphorus and zinc. The FDA warns that bone meal may contain dangerously high amounts of lead.

➤ **Dolomite.** This is a mineral also known as calcium magnesium carbonate. It contains calcium—and also magnesium, which you may not want or shouldn't take. The FDA warns that dolomite may contain dangerously high amounts of lead.

➤ **Oyster shell calcium.** Actually, this is calcium carbonate, but it's made from ground-up oyster shells. These supplements may also contain too much lead and sometimes other contaminants such as mercury and cadmium. Don't take them if you're allergic to shellfish.

Getting the Most from Calcium

Your body uses calcium around the clock, so try to space out your calcium over the day. If you can, have calcium-rich foods with every meal. If you take supplements, spread them out through the day, and don't take more than 600 mg at a time.

If milk is good and calcium supplements are good, isn't it even better to take them together? No—take them an hour or two apart so your body can absorb the most calcium from both.

Most people don't have any side effects from taking calcium supplements, even in high doses. To be on the safe side, though, don't take more than 2,000 mg of calcium in a day—that's your total intake, including food and supplements.

Sometimes people who take calcium supplements get constipation. If this happens to you, space your supplements out more across the day and be sure to drink plenty of water.

In very rare cases, too much calcium (over 2,000 mg a day for a long time) can cause hypercalcemia, or an overload of calcium in the blood. The symptoms include appetite loss, drowsiness, constipation, dry mouth, headache, and weakness. Stop taking the supplements and call your doctor.

The Dynamic Duo: Calcium and Vitamin D

Vitamin D and calcium work together to keep your blood level of calcium normal. You also need vitamin D to help your bones hold onto their calcium. For the best protection against osteoporosis, try to get about 200 IU of vitamin D daily. (Refer to Chapter 5, "Vitamin D: Soak It Up," for more information.)

Some calcium supplements also contain vitamin D. These combinations are meant only for people who don't get outside very much. Most people don't need to take extra vitamin D, because your body makes it from sunshine—and too much vitamin D from supplements can be toxic.

The dynamic duo has a sidekick: magnesium. This mineral helps you absorb calcium and use vitamin D properly. The rule of thumb is: half as much magnesium as calcium. So, if you're getting 1,000 mg of calcium a day from food and supplements, you need 500 mg of magnesium. You can get calcium supplements that also have magnesium in them, but that may not be a good idea (see Chapter 9, "Magnesium: Health Magic," for why). See the following table for other supplements to take with, or avoid taking with, calcium.

What to Take with Calcium and What to Avoid

Calcim Is Helped By	Calcium Is Blocked By
Vitamin D	Alcohol
Vitamin K	Tobacco
	Magnesium
	High-fiber foods

continues

**What to Take with Calcium and What
to Avoid   (continued)**

Calcim Is Helped By	Calcium Is Blocked By
	Foods high in oxalic acid
	Cortisone-like drugs
	Tetracycline
	Thyroid drugs
	Aluminum antacids
	Some drugs for high cholesterol

Calcium and High Blood Pressure

Calcium may help prevent or treat high blood pressure
in some people. If you don't eat much calcium, you're
more likely to get high blood pressure than someone who
gets the DRI or more. In general, the higher the level of
calcium in your blood, the lower your blood pressure.
According to one study, taking 1,000 mg a day of extra
calcium also lowers your *diastolic blood pressure* (that's the
pressure when your heart is relaxed between beats), but it
doesn't seem to do anything for your *systolic pressure*
(when your heart is contracting and the pressure is
highest).

Other studies show that taking calcium supplements (anywhere from 400 to 1,000 mg a day) can lower blood pressure for some people, especially African Americans and
people who are sensitive to salt.

If your blood pressure is on the high side but you don't
yet need medicine to lower it, take a look at your calcium
level. Try to raise your intake to at least 1,000 mg a day.
After a few months, you may notice a drop in your blood
pressure.

Pregnant women sometimes have trouble with high blood pressure. Calcium supplements seem to help. Because pregnant women need extra calcium anyway, this is another good reason to be sure you're getting 1,000 mg a day—enough for you and your growing baby.

WARNING: If you take medicine for high blood pressure, keep taking it. Talk to your doctor about calcium supplements before you try them.

Calcium and Colon Cancer

The research here is promising. In general, the lower your calcium intake, the more likely you are to get colon cancer, possibly because calcium blocks the growth of cancer cells. If you're at risk (if one of your parents had colon cancer, for example), getting 1,500 to 2,000 mg of calcium a day could help ward it off.

Calcium and Kidney Stones

For years, doctors warned patients who had kidney stones to avoid calcium. The idea was that the calcium combined with oxalate, a natural substance found in dark-green leafy vegetables such as spinach, to form the painful stones.

In fact, the opposite may be true. In a recent study, women who had the highest calcium intake were the least likely to have kidney stones. If you've ever had a kidney stone, there's no longer really much reason to give up the bone-protecting benefits of calcium. To be on the safe side, though, try to get most of your calcium from food, not supplements. If you do take supplements, take them with meals to block your uptake of oxalates. And be sure to drink plenty of water every day.

WARNING: Do not take calcium supplements if you have kidney disease!

Calcium and Heart Disease

Two important studies in 1997 pointed out a link between atherosclerosis (arteries clogged with fatty deposits called plaque) and osteoporosis. In the first study, researchers found that women who had the most bone loss from osteoporosis were also the most likely to have calcium-containing plaque blocking their carotid arteries. Because the carotid arteries carry blood to the brain, these women were at higher risk of having a stroke. The second study showed that men and women with low vitamin D levels also had higher rates of calcium-containing plaque in the arteries leading to their hearts, making them more vulnerable to heart attacks. Much more follow-up research needs to be done, of course, but these studies show how important calcium is for every aspect of your long-term health.

Chapter 9

Magnesium: Health Magic

In This Chapter

➤ Why you need magnesium

➤ Foods that are high in magnesium

➤ How magnesium helps your heart

➤ Helping your blood pressure with magnesium

➤ Magnesium helps relieve asthma

➤ How magnesium can help diabetes

Every single cell in your body needs magnesium to produce energy. You also need magnesium to make more than 300 different enzymes, to send messages along your nerves, to make your muscles relax, to maintain strong bones and teeth, help your heart beat, and to keep your blood pressure at normal levels. Magnesium seems to help some health problems, such as asthma and diabetes, and can be very valuable for treating heart rhythm problems.

You also need magnesium to use other vitamins and minerals properly. Vitamin C and calcium both work better, for example, when there's plenty of magnesium around.

To do all that, you need a fair amount of magnesium. In fact, your body contains about 25 grams (g) of magnesium. Most of it's in your bones and teeth, but you also have a lot in your muscles and blood. The amount in your blood is very important for keeping your body's functions in balance. Just as you need calcium to make your muscles contract—when your heart beats, for example—you need magnesium to make them relax again. That's why the levels of calcium and magnesium in your blood have to be steady and why you need to be sure you're getting enough of both. If you don't have enough of them, your body will pull these minerals from your bones and put them into your blood—which can lead to weakened bones.

The DRI for Magnesium

In 1989, the RDA for magnesium was lowered somewhat, especially for children and pregnant women. The reasoning was that most people were getting less than even the lowered amount, but they seemed healthy enough anyway. In 1997, the recommended amounts for magnesium were raised a little as one of the first of the new DRIs (remember those from Chapter 1, "The A to K of Nutrition"?). Here's a chart with the new guidelines:

The DRI for Magnesium

Age/Sex	Magnesium in mg
Infants	
0–0.5 year	30
0.5–1 year	75
Children	
1–3 years	80
4–8 years	130
9–13 years	240

Age/Sex	Magnesium in mg
Boys 14–18 years	410
Girls 14–18 years	360
Young Adults and Adults	
Men 19–30 years	400
Men 31+ years	420
Women 19–30 years	310
Women 31+ years	320
Pregnant Women	
18 years and under	400
19–30 years	350
31–50 years	360
Nursing Women	
18 years and under	360
19–30 years	310
31–50 years	320

Although the new DRI is higher than the old RDA, many researchers believe it's still too low to prevent some health problems.

The research into the value of larger doses is now pretty solid. Many nutritionists and doctors now suggest 500 mg a day for adults. This amount could do a lot to help keep your blood pressure normal and prevent heart disease.

Eating Your Magnesium

Magnesium is found in lots of foods. Good sources include nuts, beans, dark-green leafy vegetables (of course), whole grains, and seafood. Most people get a lot of their daily magnesium from milk, which has about 34 mg per cup. Soy foods such as miso and tofu (bean curd) are high in magnesium; soymilk actually has more magnesium than cow's milk. There isn't much magnesium in meat or foods that have been refined or processed a lot—just compare the 23 mg in a slice of whole-wheat bread to the measly 5 mg in a slice of white bread.

Now You're Cooking

You now have an extra good reason for eating that double-fudge brownie: Chocolate is high in magnesium! Here's how much: ¹/₄ cup of chocolate chips = 35 mg; 1 ounce of unsweetened baking chocolate = 88 mg; 1 tablespoon of unsweetened cocoa powder = 25 mg.

Getting the Most from Magnesium

It's not that easy to get the RDA for magnesium just from your food—and it's even harder to get 500 mg a day that way. Even so, that's the best way to get your magnesium, along with all the other valuable vitamins and minerals also found in magnesium-rich foods.

If you want to take a supplement, remember that your daily multi supplement probably has 10 to 50 mg of magnesium. Between your food and your multi, you won't need a large dose of supplemental magnesium to make up the difference. That's good, because large doses of magnesium—over 600 mg—can give you diarrhea.

The magnesium in supplements is always combined with some other harmless substance to make it stable. At the vitamin counter you'll find a lot of different choices, with names like magnesium orotate and magnesium gluconate.

We suggest taking magnesium aspartate, magnesium glycinate, or magnesium citrate, because you absorb these the best. For the most benefit, take between 200 and 500 mg a day; don't go over 500 mg. Spread your magnesium out over the day and take the supplements with meals. If you get diarrhea from the supplements, cut back on your dose. If you have kidney problems of any sort, talk to your doctor before you try magnesium supplements.

WARNING: Do not take magnesium supplements or ant-acids containing magnesium if you also take the antibiotic drugs Cipro® or tetracycline! The magnesium will block the drugs from entering your bloodstream! If you take pre-scription *diuretics,* insulin, or digitalis, you may need more magnesium. Discuss magnesium supplements with your doctor before you try them!

What's in a Word?

Diuretic drugs make your kidneys produce more urine, which removes water—and also some minerals and vitamins—from your body. Prescription diuretics such as furosemide (Lasix®) are mostly used to treat high blood pressure. These drugs don't usually lower your magnesium level, although they may affect your potassium level.

Magnesium and Your Heart

Low levels of magnesium seem to be related to some types of heart problems. Because magnesium helps your muscles relax, a shortage may cause a spasm in one of your coro-nary arteries. The spasm blocks the blood flow and can cause a heart attack. Some doctors think that a shortage of magnesium is behind many sudden heart attacks, especially in people who don't have a history of heart disease. In fact, intravenous magnesium is used in emergency rooms as a treatment for heart attacks.

Magnesium may also protect against heart attacks caused by blood clots. Magnesium helps keep the clots from forming by making your platelets (tiny blood cells that form clots) less "sticky." This makes them less likely to lump together into an artery-clogging clot.

Too little magnesium can also cause *cardiac arrhythmias*. When that happens, your heart beats irregularly. You might skip a beat or have an extra one, or your heart could beat too fast. If the problem is serious enough, your heartbeat doesn't quickly return to normal and you could die suddenly. Studies suggest that people with low levels of magnesium are more likely to die suddenly from heart rhythm problems.

What's in a Word?

Cardiac arrhythmias make your heart beat irregularly. Sometimes the arrhythmmia makes you have an extra heartbeat or skip one; it could also make your heart beat too fast. Cardiac arrhythmias can be serious. See your doctor at once if you're having symptoms.

WARNING: Do not take magnesium supplements or antacids containing magnesium if you have congestive heart failure!

Magnesium Manages Blood Pressure

Magnesium helps your muscles relax. If you don't have enough magnesium, the walls of your blood vessels could tighten up, which raises your blood pressure. As it turns out, many people with high blood pressure don't eat enough magnesium. When they get more in their diet— up to 600 mg a day—their blood pressure drops. This doesn't work for everybody, though, so we can't say for sure that magnesium will make your high blood pressure go down. Even so, many doctors suggest that you try eating more magnesium-rich foods if you have high blood pressure. You could also try taking 400 mg a day in supplements, but talk to your doctor first.

Pregnant women sometimes get dangerously high blood pressure, especially in the last few months of the pregnancy. Magnesium may help prevent this problem. If you're pregnant, your doctor will probably prescribe a multi supplement that has magnesium in it. Don't take additional magnesium supplements unless your doctor recommends them.

Help for Asthma

When you have an asthma attack, the muscles lining the airways in your lungs contract. This makes the airways get too narrow, so you have trouble breathing. Magnesium helps the muscles relax, so the airways open up and you can breathe more easily. In emergency rooms, intravenous magnesium is used to treat severe asthma attacks. Don't try to treat an attack on your own by swallowing magnesium supplements, though—it doesn't work and could be dangerous. Take your medicine instead.

If you have asthma, it might be because your diet is low in magnesium. Getting more through supplements and magnesium-rich foods—up to 1,000 mg a day—could help prevent attacks and make your attacks less severe. For the best results, spread the dose out over the day.

WARNING: Even mild asthma is a serious health problem, because it can suddenly get much worse. If you already take medicine for asthma—even nonprescription drugs—don't stop! Talk to your doctor about taking magnesium and other supplements before you try them.

Magnesium and Diabetes

High blood pressure is often a problem for people with diabetes—and people with diabetes often have low magnesium levels. Is there a connection? Some doctors think there is and recommend magnesium supplements for diabetic patients. Magnesium may also help diabetics control their blood sugar better and help prevent complications later on, like eye problems and heart disease. There's also some evidence that older people who are at risk for diabetes can prevent it by taking extra magnesium. If you have diabetes or are at risk for it, try to get as much magnesium as you can from your diet and consider taking between 200 and 300 mg a day in supplements. Talk to your doctor about taking supplements before you try them, especially if you have kidney problems because of your diabetes.

Magnesium for Healthy Bones

We talked a lot about the importance of calcium for strong bones in the previous chapter. But calcium isn't the only mineral you need to keep your bones healthy—you also need enough magnesium. The magnesium helps keep your calcium levels in balance and makes sure you produce enough vitamin D.

The general rule of thumb is that you need twice as much calcium as magnesium to prevent osteoporosis. Because women need more calcium as they get older, they also need more magnesium. According to the NIH, women ages 25 to 50 need 1,000 mg of calcium a day, so they also need to get 500 mg of magnesium. If you're a woman over age 50 and you're not taking estrogen, you probably need

1,500 mg of calcium and 750 mg of magnesium every day. This amount is hard to get through your diet alone—consider taking magnesium and calcium supplements.

Magnesium and Migraines

People who get migraine headaches often have low magnesium levels. Does that mean that low magnesium causes migraines? Could be, although we're still not sure why. If you get migraines, try to get 500 mg of magnesium a day through your diet and by taking a magnesium supplement. This daily amount could reduce the number of attacks you get. It seems to work particularly well as a preventive for women who get migraines as part of their menstrual cycle.

One very interesting recent study showed that in about half the cases, intravenous magnesium stopped migraine headaches in their tracks. Unfortunately, once you have a migraine, just swallowing magnesium supplements doesn't have the same effect.

Other Problems Helped by Magnesium

There's a lot of controversy over whether magnesium helps some other health problems. We're not too sure about some of these—magnesium doesn't seem to do anything for prostate trouble, gallstones, body odor (we'll never understand how that one got started), or depression, for example, although some people claim it does. Let's look at two cases where the evidence shows that magnesium helps:

➤ **Premenstrual syndrome (PMS).** Some women swear that magnesium supplements relieve uncomfortable PMS symptoms, especially breast tenderness, headaches, and irritability. If you get severe PMS, try taking 300 to 500 mg a day for the two weeks leading up to your period. If you get severe cramps from your period, keep taking the magnesium during that time—it may help reduce cramping. Magnesium may help even more if you combine it with pyridoxine (refer to Chapter 3, "B Healthy," for more information about this).

➤ **Preventing kidney stones.** Magnesium supplements seem to help keep calcium kidney stones from coming back. All you need is 100 to 300 mg a day. The magnesium seems to help more if you also take 10 mg of pyridoxine (vitamin B_6) a day. If you get kidney stones, talk to your doctor about magnesium supplements before you try them.

There's also some interesting evidence suggesting that magnesium plays a role in preventing cancer. The strongest argument for this is that cancer rates seem to be higher in areas where magnesium levels in the soil and water are naturally low.

WARNING: Do not take magnesium supplements or antacids containing magnesium if you have kidney disease!

Chapter 10

Zinc: Put Some Zip in Your System

In This Chapter

➤ Why you need zinc

➤ Foods that are high in zinc

➤ How zinc helps colds

➤ How zinc helps prostate problems

➤ Why you need zinc for healthy skin, hair, and nails

Over 200 different enzymes in your body depend on zinc to work properly. You also need zinc to make many hormones, including the ones that tell your immune system what to do when you're under attack from germs. Zinc is essential for making the hormones that control growth and for the important male hormone testosterone. You have some zinc in every one of your body's cells, but most of it is in your skin, hair, nails, and eyes—and in your prostate gland if you're male. All told, your body contains just over 2.2 g of zinc.

The RDA for Zinc

Even though you use zinc in many important body processes, you don't need to eat much of it. Technically speaking, zinc is a trace element—a mineral you need in only very small amounts. (We'll talk more about trace elements in Chapter 12, "The Trace Minerals: A Little Goes a Long Way.") The adult RDA for zinc is 15 mg a day or less—an amount that most everybody easily gets from food. Check out the following table to see what your zinc need is.

The RDA for Zinc

Age/Sex	Zinc in mg
Infants	
0–1 year	5
Children	
1–10 years	10
Adolescents and Adults	
Males 11+ years	15
Females 11+ years	12
Pregnant women	15
Nursing women	19

The first hint that zinc is an important nutrient came almost a century ago in Egypt, when doctors noticed that poor young boys who ate almost nothing but unleavened bread were very short and underdeveloped. It turned out that their diet had very little zinc. Once they got more zinc in their diet, they started growing normally again.

Eating Your Zinc

The best food source of zinc by far is oysters. There are about 12 mg in a single raw oyster. Other foods that are good sources of zinc are lean meat, poultry, and organ meats. You only absorb about 10 percent of the zinc you get from animal foods, and you absorb even less from the zinc in plant foods.

Now You're Cooking

Did you know pure maple syrup is a good source of zinc? There's 0.8 mg in 1 tablespoon.

There's a fair amount of zinc in beans, nuts, seeds, and whole grains, but your body can't use it very well. That's because these foods also have a lot of fiber. A substance called phytic acid in the fiber combines with zinc and keeps a lot of it from being absorbed. Fruits are low in zinc.

Getting the Most from Zinc

You have a lot of choices at the vitamin counter when you're looking for a zinc supplement. What you want is a form that you can easily absorb, so we suggest zinc gluconate. Zinc picolinate, zinc citrate, or zinc monomethionate are also good options.

Most good multi supplements have the RDA for zinc. If you want to get more, try zinc supplements; they usually come in 10, 30, or 50 mg capsules. Zinc supplements in large amounts can block your absorption of calcium, copper, and iron. It's especially important to keep your copper and zinc levels in balance. If you regularly take extra zinc, be sure you're also getting some extra copper.

WARNING: Do not take zinc if you are taking the antibiotic drug tetracycline. The zinc will keep the tetracycline from being absorbed into your bloodstream.

Fighting Off Colds

The next time you catch a cold, zinc could help you get over it quicker. Your immune system needs zinc to work at top efficiency. In fact, your infection-fighting white blood cells contain a lot of the zinc in your body. Giving them a zinc boost when you have a cold seems to help them fight off the virus faster. It also seems to reduce cold symptoms such as a runny nose, coughing, and hoarseness.

For treating a cold with zinc, the best approach seems to be lozenges made of zinc gluconate with glycine. Put the lozenge in your mouth and let it dissolve slowly. Don't chew it or swallow it. Repeat every two hours or so for one or two days only. Adults shouldn't take more than 12 lozenges a day. Limit children to no more than six a day. You can buy zinc lozenges in any health-food store; many pharmacies now carry them as well. Most lozenges contain 22 or 23 mg—anything less won't help you very much. Just swallowing zinc supplements won't help your cold symptoms at all.

There are some drawbacks to zinc lozenges. Even though they're flavored to disguise their awful taste, they can leave a bad aftertaste in your mouth. If you take a lot of them they can affect your sense of taste and smell—but your senses should return to normal a few days after you stop taking the extra zinc.

Zinc may be a very useful immune system booster in general. It seems to give a real boost to your *thymus gland*, especially if you're over age 40. By then, your thymus may have naturally shrunk quite a bit, so it's not producing the hormones it used to—and those hormones stimulate your body to produce infection-fighting blood cells. Getting a little extra zinc—just 15 to 30 mg—every day may get your thymus moving again. That means your immune system will work better and fight off illness faster.

What's in a Word?

Your **thymus gland** is a small organ in your neck just above your breastbone. It makes some of the hormones that tell your immune system what to do. When you're born, your thymus is quite large. By the time you're 40, it's shrunk quite a bit. Recent studies show that zinc can revitalize your thymus and get it working again.

Zinc Club for Men

Are the guys just kidding around when they tell you to eat oysters for a better sex life? Believe it or not, they're right. Oysters are by far the food highest in zinc—and you need plenty of zinc to make testosterone and other male hormones. You also need zinc to make healthy sperm and semen, so getting more zinc in your diet could help solve male infertility.

Zinc can also be very helpful for treating and possibly even preventing prostate problems, especially a condition called *benign prostatic hypertrophy* (*BPH*). A healthy prostate gland naturally has a lot of zinc in it, but men with BPH often have low zinc levels. Taking an extra 50 mg a day of zinc supplements seems to help some men with mild BPH by shrinking the prostate. It takes a while for the zinc to kick in—stay with the supplements for three to six months before you decide they're not working.

Finally, guys, despite rumors to the contrary, zinc doesn't stop balding or restore lost hair.

What's in a Word?

A small male organ called the prostate gland wraps around the urethra, the tube that carries urine from your kidneys to your bladder. As males get older (especially when over age 50), the prostate may enlarge and start pressing on the urethra, a condition called **benign prostatic hypertrophy (BPH)**. The main symptom is the need to urinate frequently.

Healthy Skin, Nails, and Hair

Zinc is really important for healthy skin. A shortage of zinc is often behind minor skin rashes and irritations that don't seem to have any real cause. These often clear up when patients start eating a diet higher in zinc or take zinc supplements. Zinc also sometimes helps people with psoriasis.

Sometimes a zinc shortage causes white spots on the fingernails or nails that break easily. Adding zinc to your diet could clear up the problem.

Zinc for Healing

Zinc is essential for healing wounds. Several studies have shown that patients recovering from surgery heal faster if they get enough zinc. The effect is dramatic if the patient was low on zinc to begin with; it didn't work as well on patients who had good zinc levels. If you're scheduled for an operation, talk to your doctor about taking zinc supplements for a few weeks before and after. It could make a difference in how quickly you recover.

Think Zinc for Other Problems

Some zinc zanies recommend it for all sorts of health problems. Here are some ways zinc may make a difference:

➤ **Diabetes.** Some diabetics may be too low on zinc because they don't absorb it well and also excrete it quickly. Zinc supplements could help. Zinc might also help with two other problems diabetics often have: slow wound healing and frequent infections.

➤ **Macular degeneration.** This serious eye problem is the leading cause of blindness in the elderly. Your eyes naturally contain a lot of zinc—and a lot of it is concentrated in your retina, the part of your eye affected by macular degeneration. Zinc supplements could help prevent or slow down vision loss from macular degeneration.

➤ **Memory.** Can't remember where you left the car keys? Maybe you're not getting enough zinc. People who get the RDA do better on memory tests than those who don't.

Does zinc help Alzheimer's disease, rheumatoid arthritis, anorexia, or liver disease? Does it prevent cancer? Probably not, but we don't know for sure—the information in all cases is contradictory.

Chapter 11

Electrolytes: The Elements of Good Health

In This Chapter

➤ Why potassium, sodium, and chloride are vital to your health

➤ Why you need to keep your electrolytes in balance

➤ How sodium raises your blood pressure and how potassium lowers it

➤ How potassium can prevent strokes

Electrolytes are minerals that dissolve in water and carry electrical charges. In your body, potassium, sodium, and chloride are the electrolyte minerals. And since you're made mostly of water, these minerals are found everywhere in your body: inside your cells, in the spaces between cells, in your blood, in your lymph, and everywhere else. Each tiny particle of sodium and potassium in your body has a positive charge; each tiny particle of chloride has a negative one. Because electrolytes have electrical charges, they can move easily back and forth through your cell membranes. Why is that so important? Because as they move into a cell, they carry other nutrients with them and as they move out, they carry out waste products and excess water.

Potassium, sodium, and chloride are very closely linked—so closely that we really can't talk about them separately. Here's why: To keep your body in balance, your cells need to have a lot of potassium inside them and a lot of sodium in the fluids outside them. To keep the balance, sodium and potassium constantly move back and forth through your cell membranes.

You can see the link between sodium and potassium. Where does the chloride come in? Sodium combines easily with other elements. Here's a good example: Remember that familiar formula NaCl from science class? Na is the chemical symbol for sodium, while Cl means chloride. Put them together and you have sodium chloride, better known as ordinary table salt. You mostly need the sodium found in salt (table salt is about 40 percent sodium), but your body also needs the chloride. Among other things, you use it to make hydrochloric acid, the powerful digestive juice in your stomach.

Why You Need Electrolytes

All three electrolytes—potassium, sodium, and chloride—keep the amount of water in your body in balance, carry impulses along your nerves, help make your muscles contract and relax, and keep your body from becoming too acidic or alkaline. You need electrolytes to carry glucose (blood sugar) and other nutrients into your cells and to carry waste products and extra water out again. Electrolytes also regulate your blood pressure and your heartbeat. In fact, sodium and potassium are so important for controlling your blood pressure that we'll talk about that more later on in this chapter.

The RDAs for Electrolytes

Now that you know how important electrolytes are for keeping you alive, here's a surprise: There are no RDAs for them. Why? Every single living cell on earth—plant or animal—needs potassium, sodium, and chloride, which means that there's plenty of them in your food. Because the electrolytes are so easy to eat, nobody ever really gets deficient. By the logic of the RDAs, then, there's no reason to bother setting a minimum amount, since everybody gets whatever it is anyway. It makes sense—and as we'll explain later on in this chapter, too much sodium, not too little, is a much bigger health problem.

Even though there aren't any RDAs for potassium, sodium, and chloride, there are estimates of the minimum amounts you need to have. When you look at the following table, you'll see that the amounts are really pretty small.

Estimated Minimum Requirements for Potassium, Sodium, and Chloride

Age	Potassium in mg	Sodium in mg	Chloride in mg
Infants			
0–0.5 year	500	120	180
0.5–1 year	700	200	300
Children and Adults			
1 year	1,000	225	350
2–5 years	1,400	300	500
6–9 years	1,600	400	600
10+ years	2,000	500	750

For the sake of comparison, figure there's about 3,000 mg of sodium in a teaspoon of salt. To stay healthy, you need to get less than $1/4$ teaspoon of salt every day. Many researchers think the sodium requirement is on the high side and that you can be perfectly healthy on only 200 mg (about $1/15$ a teaspoon) a day.

WARNING: People with kidney disease must avoid sodium and potassium! Follow your doctor's instructions!

Eating Your Electrolytes

Potassium is found in almost all foods, including fruits, vegetables, beans, meat, milk, and grains. We don't recommend taking potassium supplements unless your doctor prescribes them for you. If you want to get an easy potassium boost, eat a banana or have a glass of orange juice.

Some sodium and chloride are found in almost all foods. We get plenty of both in the form of sodium chloride—the chemical name for plain old table salt.

Shaking Up Salt

Everybody tells you to eat less salt, but it's hard to avoid. We sprinkle salt on our food as a seasoning and it is added to almost every processed food. Condiments like ketchup and soy sauce are loaded with salt. Baked goods made with sodium bicarbonate are full of sodium. And you can tell from their names that many food additives, like monosodium glutamate (MSG) and sodium nitrite, have a lot of sodium. In fact, salt is so common that the typical American diet contains between 10 and 15 times the RDA for sodium, or between 5,000 and 7,500 mg, or between almost 2 and 4 teaspoons of salt every day. Cutting back on salt could reduce your chances of high blood pressure, stroke, kidney problems, and heart disease. It's an easy way to improve your health.

Quack, Quack

If you sweat a lot from an athletic activity or hard work in hot weather, drink plain water instead of those expensive sports drinks. It's important to replace the lost fluid. If you want to replace the lost potassium, have a piece of fruit or some OJ—there's over 500 mg in a cup.

Electrifying News on High Blood Pressure

The balance between your potassium and sodium levels is important for keeping your blood pressure down. Many researchers believe that a good balance is roughly five parts potassium or even more to one part sodium. Unfortunately, our high-salt diets give many of us balances that are more like one part potassium to two parts sodium, or twice as much sodium as potassium. It's not surprising that one in four American adults—some 50 million people—has high blood pressure. Among adults over age 65, more than half have high blood pressure.

Now You're Cooking

Salt substitutes swap sodium chloride for potassium chloride. Give them a try, but only to season your food at the table. Using potassium chloride for cooking gives food a bitter taste. If you need to restrict your potassium, don't use salt substitutes—most have well over 600 mg in $1/4$ teaspoon.

About 10 percent of the people who have high blood pressure are salt sensitive—sodium in their diet makes their blood pressure zoom up. These people should try very hard to reduce their sodium intake. Older people and African Americans are most likely to be salt sensitive, but it makes sense for everyone to cut back. Studies show that overall, the average person who consumes less salt has lower blood pressure. In fact, a 1997 study in the prestigious British medical journal *The Lancet* suggests that older people who lower their salt intake also sharply lower their risk of stroke, even if they don't have high blood pressure.

Just cutting back on sodium isn't the whole solution. Many people with high blood pressure also benefit from *increasing* their potassium. When they do, they get a more natural balance in their electrolytes, and their blood pressure goes down. You don't need pills or supplements to get the benefits: Just eating fewer salty foods and more foods rich in potassium will help. In many cases, lowering your sodium intake to under 2,000 mg a day and raising your potassium intake to over 3,500 mg a day has a very beneficial effect, especially for older people.

Proof that this works came in 1997 as part of the important Dietary Approaches to Stop Hypertension (DASH) study. Some people in the study ate a typical American diet; others ate a diet that was much lower in fat and much higher in fruits and vegetables—which are high in potassium. All the people in the study got about 3,000 mg a day of sodium but the people who ate the typical American diet got only 1,700 mg of potassium, while the people who ate lots more fruits and vegetables got about 4,700 mg of potassium. Guess whose blood pressure dropped? You're right. The typical Americans didn't improve at all, but the fruit and vegetable eaters saw their blood pressure drop substantially. And the higher their blood pressure was to begin with, the more it dropped.

Preventing Strokes with Potassium

Even if you don't have high blood pressure, potassium could help protect you against having a stroke. If your potassium intake is low, your odds of a stroke go up, no matter what other risk factors you may have, such a cigarette smoking or being overweight. According to one long-term study of older adults, just one daily serving of a potassium-rich food could cut your risk of a stroke by an amazing 40 percent. That's just one banana, glass of orange juice, or baked potato. And if you eat more than one serving a day, your odds against a stroke might improve even more.

Chapter 12

The Trace Minerals: A Little Goes a Long Way

In This Chapter

➤ What trace minerals are and why you need them

➤ The roles of iron, iodine, chromium, and selenium

➤ The roles of boron, copper, manganese, molybdenum, and other less-important trace minerals

➤ Trace minerals you should avoid

If you have less than 1 teaspoon of a mineral in your body, it's a trace mineral—one that you need, but only in very small amounts. In the human body, 15 substances are considered necessary trace minerals (check out the following table for the whole list).

Although you need all the trace minerals, some are more important than others. Zinc, for example, is so important that we gave it its own chapter (see Chapter 10, "Zinc: Put Some Zip in Your System"). Some of the other trace minerals, like nickel, are so minor and so easy to get from your food that there just isn't a lot to say about them.

We'll concentrate on the trace minerals that could make a real difference to your health. Not every trace mineral has an RDA or even a Safe and Adequate Intake (SAI) amount. We just don't know about some of them, like nickel and boron.

The Trace Minerals

Mineral	Function	RDA or SAI
Boron	Builds healthy bones	None
Chromium	Controls blood sugar	50–200 mcg
Cobalt	Needed for cobalamin (vitamin B$_{12}$)	None
Copper	Needed for antioxidant enzymes, red blood cells, and other enzymes	1.5–3.0 mg
Fluoride	Protects against tooth decay and builds healthy bones	1.5–4.0 mg
Iodine	Needed for thyroid hormones	150 mcg
Iron	Needed for hemoglobin in red blood cells	10–15 mg
Manganese	Needed for protein digestion and tissue formation	2.5–5.0 mg
Molybdenum	Normal growth and development	75–250 mcg
Nickel	Needed to make some enzymes and hormones	None
Selenium	Needed for antioxidant enzyme glutathione	55–70 mcg
Silicon	Builds healthy bones	None

Mineral	Function	RDA or SAI
Tin	Unknown	None
Vanadium	Unknown	None
Zinc	Building a healthy immune system	12–15 mg

Why You Need Trace Minerals

You might not need much of a trace mineral, but some are especially important when it comes to making the many different enzymes, hormones, and other chemical messengers your body uses every minute of every day. You need iodine to make thyroid hormones, which in turn control some very important parts of your metabolism, including your body weight. You need the trace mineral iron to carry oxygen in your blood and also to make other enzymes. Some trace minerals, such as selenium, are used to make the powerful natural antioxidants that protect you against free radicals. And some trace minerals work closely with vitamins to make them more active and long-lasting.

We still don't completely understand the roles of some other trace minerals, such as manganese. We know that you'll get health problems if you don't get the tiny amount you need, but we're still not sure why.

RDAs and Safe and Adequate Intakes

In general, you need to be cautious about trace minerals. The toxic amount of a trace mineral often isn't that much higher than the safe amount. The adult RDA for selenium, for example, is between 55 and 70 mcg. The toxic amount is about 600 mcg, or less than 10 times the RDA. Likewise, too much iron can be more harmful than too little.

Most people get plenty of all the trace minerals from their food and don't need to take supplements. If you feel you need more of a particular trace element, try to get it from your food whenever possible.

Most good daily multi supplements contain at least some of the trace minerals. The amounts vary—read the labels. A lot of multi supplements contain at least the RDA for iron. As we'll discuss a little further on, this may not be a good idea for some people. Again, read the label carefully.

Sometimes combination supplements contain one or two trace elements that are especially important. For example, calcium supplements sometimes come with magnesium and boron, because these two minerals are needed to build healthy bones. These supplements are on the expensive side. Do you really need the trace minerals as well? Probably not, especially if you also take a daily multi supplement.

There may be times when you want to take additional supplements of a particular trace mineral. Be very cautious here—take the smallest possible dose. Too much of a trace mineral could be as harmful as too little. Whenever possible, try to get your trace minerals from your food instead of pills.

Iron: Basic for Blood

Iron barely qualifies as a trace mineral, because you have just under a teaspoon of it in your body. You need it chiefly to carry oxygen in your blood. Every one of your red blood cells contains a protein called *hemoglobin*—and four atoms of iron are attached to every hemoglobin molecule. In your lungs, oxygen molecules attach to the iron atoms and are carried to your cells. When the oxygen reaches its destination, it's swapped for the waste carbon dioxide and carried back to your lungs. You get rid of it by exhaling.

What's in a Word?

Hemoglobin is the oxygen-carrying protein that gives your red blood cells their color. Every molecule of hemoglobin has four atoms of iron in it.

How much iron you have determines how much oxygen gets to the rest of your body. Not enough iron, and you start making fewer red blood cells. Not enough red blood cells, and you become anemic—weak, tired, pale, short of breath.

Just how common is "iron-poor blood"? Not as common as all the advertising says, but common enough to be concerned. You could be low on iron for a long time before you become anemic. An important 1997 study found that 1 out of 10 American women and small children were deficient in iron—or about 700,000 toddlers and 7.8 million women! Of those, about 240,000 toddlers and 3.3 million women were anemic. The results were so shocking that a national screening program for iron deficiency is being considered.

The RDA for iron was lowered in 1989, once again showing that the RDAs are bare minimums and far from ideal—especially for women. Many doctors now suggest getting at least the RDA for men and closer to 20 mg a day for women. In general, that level or even a much larger dose—up to 75 mg a day—is quite safe.

Eating Your Iron
The average American diet has about 6 mg of iron for every 1,000 calories you eat. That means you need to eat

about 2,500 calories a day to get enough iron. Because women generally eat less than 2,000 calories a day, you need to be extra sure you're getting enough iron by choosing iron-rich foods.

Now You're Cooking

Foods cooked in cast-iron cookware absorb safe, tasteless amounts of extra iron. Acidic foods absorb the most. Tomato sauce simmered in a cast-iron pot could have as much as 300 times the iron as sauce simmered in an aluminum pot.

Iron is found in many common foods. It falls into two categories: *heme iron,* found in meat, and *nonheme iron,* found in plant foods. Rich sources of heme iron include organ meats, lean beef, chicken, oysters, and pork. Good sources of nonheme iron are whole grains, peas, beans, spinach, nuts, and blackstrap (unrefined) molasses. One of the best sources of iron is cream of wheat cereal—there's over 7 mg in 6 ounces. Many cold breakfast cereals such as bran flakes also have plenty of iron, both naturally and from added supplements.

Too much iron in your system can be as big a problem as too little. The excess iron oxidizes, causing damaging free radicals that have been implicated in heart disease and cancer. We suggest getting your iron from your food and taking supplements only if you're anemic or your doctor recommend them for some other reason.

Iodine: Important for the Thyroid

You need iodine to make the *thyroid* hormones that regulate your body's metabolism. In fact, that's all iodine does for you, but it's a lot: Those thyroid hormones play a big role in your growth, cell reproduction, nerve functions, and how your cells use oxygen. One of the hormones, thyroxin, regulates how fast you use the energy from your food. If you don't have enough iodine, your thyroid swells up in an effort to make more hormones, a condition called *hypothyroidism*. The swelling is called a *goiter*.

What's in a Word?

Your **thyroid** is a small butterfly shaped gland found in your neck just below your Adam's apple. It produces hormones, including one called thyroxin that regulates your metabolism. A shortage of iodine can lead to **hypothryoidism,** or underactive thyroid. When that happens, your thyroid gland swells up and forms a lump in your neck called a **goiter.**

Iodine is added to a lot of daily multi supplements, but it's not really needed. Since 1924, American salt producers have been adding iodine to table salt at the rate of 400 mcg per teaspoon. That's enough to be sure just about everyone will get plenty of iodine from the salt in their food.

Chromium: Boon for Diabetics?

One of the hottest supplements today is chromium picolinate. Diabetics swear it helps them control their blood sugar better. Body builders swear it helps them build muscle faster. Some people claim it helps lower high cholesterol, while others claim it boosts your production of the anti-aging hormone DHEA.

Let's start with how much chromium you really need. Nobody knows. The SAI range for adults is anywhere between 50 and 200 mcg. Why do you need it? In ways we still don't fully understand, chromium is involved with using fats, proteins, and carbohydrates. It's also needed to help the hormone insulin deliver glucose to your cells.

Because of the insulin connection, chromium does seem to help some people with Type II, or adult-onset, diabetes, get glucose into their cells better. We suggest you skip chromium supplements and try to get between 50 and 200 mcg a day from your food. If you decide to try supplements, talk to your doctor first and keep a close eye on your blood sugar.

What about all those other things chromium is supposed to do? There's not a lot of evidence to back up the cholesterol or DHEA claims. The body builders may be disappointed, too. The studies that showed chromium helps you lose fat and build muscle were badly flawed, and researchers haven't been able to reproduce them.

It's relatively easy to get at least 50 mcg of chromium a day from your food. Apples, broccoli, barley, corn, beef, eggs, nuts, mushrooms, oysters, rhubarb, tomatoes, and sweet potatoes are all good food sources. Most good daily multi supplements also have some chromium in them. If you decide to take a chromium supplement to help your diabetes, choose chromium glycinate or the patented type of trivalent chromium picolinate called Chromax-II GTF.

Selenium: An Essential Element

Your body's most abundant natural antioxidant is an enzyme called glutathione peroxidase—but without selenium, you can't make glutathione. A recent major study has shown that selenium can be a powerful cancer-prevention supplement. People in the study took 200 mcg of selenium daily to see if their skin cancer rate would drop. It didn't—but their rates of colorectal, lung, and prostate cancer went down sharply.

Selenium may also help protect you against heart disease. It also helps your immune system work effectively and helps remove heavy metals such as lead from your body. Vitamin E works better and longer in your body when you have plenty of selenium. All that makes selenium pretty important for a mineral you need only in micrograms.

Animal foods such as organ meats, seafood, lean meat, and chicken are all good sources of selenium. Whole grains such as oatmeal and brown rice are good plant sources of selenium, especially if they were grown in selenium-rich soil.

The benefits of selenium for cancer prevention and other health problems seem to kick in only at 200 mcg a day, though, so you may want to consider supplements. We suggest yeast-based supplements, made from yeast grown in a selenium-enriched medium. You need to be very cautious with selenium supplements. In amounts greater than 600 mcg a day, selenium can be toxic, although 200 mcg a day seems to be quite safe.

Copper: Crucial for Your Circulation

Copper is involved in a lot of body processes, but its main functions are to help keep your heart and blood vessels healthy. You need copper to make an enzyme that keeps your arteries flexible—if you don't get enough, they could rupture. You also need copper to make the insulating sheath that covers your nerves. Copper works with iron to keep your red blood cells healthy. It's also very important for making the natural antioxidant superoxide dismutase (SOD).

Copper is found in a lot of common foods. There's over 2 mg of copper in a single oyster; other shellfish, such as lobster, are also good sources. Other good foods for copper include nuts, avocados, potatoes, organ meats, whole grains, and beans and peas. You may also be getting some from your drinking water if it goes through copper pipes. Copper is also found in most good daily multi supplements.

It's important to keep your zinc and copper levels in balance, because the two minerals compete with each other to be absorbed into your body. Most nutritionists recommend a ratio of 10 parts zinc to 1 part copper. In other words, if you're taking 30 mg of zinc, be sure to take 3 mg of copper as well—but don't take more than that.

Manganese: Mystery Metal

Until 1972, when the first case came up, we didn't even know you could have a shortage of manganese. This mineral is still pretty mysterious. It seems to do a lot of the same things as magnesium, like help make your connective tissue, clot your blood, move glucose around your system, and digest your proteins. It may also be an antioxidant.

Foods that are high in manganese include tea, raisins, pineapple, spinach, broccoli, oranges, nuts, blueberries, beans, and whole grains.

Manganese can be very helpful for women with heavy menstrual flows. Eating more foods rich in manganese every day helps reduce the flow. Manganese is also an important mineral for building strong bones. If you don't get enough, you could be at greater risk for osteoporosis. The best way to get more manganese is to eat more foods that contain it. Many daily multi supplements also contain manganese. Don't overdo, though—too much manganese can interfere with your iron absorption.

Molybdenum: Making Enzymes

All of your tissues contain tiny amounts of molybdenum. It's needed to make several enzymes, particularly one called xanthine oxidase. You need this enzyme to grow and develop normally and to use iron in your body properly.

The amount of molybdenum in your food depends on where it was grown. The soil in some parts of the country is much higher in molybdenum than others. In general, good food sources include whole grains, lean meat, organ meats, beans, dark-green leafy vegetables, and milk. Most people get plenty from their food and don't need extra, although molybdenum is often found in daily multi supplements.

Quack, Quack

Sorry guys—no matter what you've heard in the locker room—molybdenum doesn't prevent impotence.

Other Trace Minerals

Did you know your body contains very tiny amounts of gold and silver? It does, but we have no idea why or what—if anything—would happen if you didn't have them. We do know why you have some other important trace minerals, though, so we'll run down the list and tell you the basics for each one.

➤ **Boron.** In the mid-1980s, researchers discovered that you need small amounts of boron to help you absorb calcium into your bones and keep it there.

How much boron is still up in the air. There's no RDA or SAI yet, but many nutritionists today suggest getting 3 mg a day. That's not a problem, because most people get 2 to 5 mg a day from their food. Good dietary sources of boron are fruits, especially apples, pears, peaches, grapes, dates, and raisins. Nuts and beans are also high in boron.

➤ **Cobalt.** Remember our discussion of cobalamin (vitamin B_{12})? You need cobalt to make this vitamin, which is essential for making red blood cells. In fact, that's *all* you need cobalt for. And because you don't need much cobalamin, you don't need much cobalt—a few micrograms is ample. If you're getting enough cobalamin from your food or supplements, you're getting plenty of cobalt.

➤ **Nickel.** We still don't know what nickel is doing in your body, although it's probably involved with making some enzymes, hormones, and cell membranes. Too much nickel is associated with cancer, heart disease, and skin problems, but there's no known effects of too little nickel. Because you absorb very, very little nickel from your food, getting too much is almost impossible. Good food sources of nickel include chocolate, whole grains, nuts, beans, fruits, and vegetables.

➤ **Silicon.** You need silicon to make your bones, cartilage, and connective tissue. Nobody's ever been deficient in silicon because it's found in many foods, especially seafood, whole grains, root vegetables such as potatoes, and beans. Silicon supplements made from the horsetail plant are said to help your nails, hair, bones, and even arteries. Skip them— they're worthless.

➤ **Tin.** You've got this in your body, but we don't know what it does. This is one trace mineral you definitely don't have to think about.

➤ **Vanadium.** Recently a lot of vanadium products have come on the market, along with a lot of hype. Some of the ads even claim it "cures" diabetes. Don't believe it. Any possible benefit vanadium might have on your blood sugar is outweighed by its possible dangers even in moderate doses. There's no known need for vanadium in your body.

Minerals You Should Miss

There are some minerals that are okay in trace amounts but definitely not okay beyond that. Here's the rundown:

Quack, Quack

A few years back researchers found aluminum in the brains of people with Alzheimer's disease. This gave rise to the rumor that food cooked in aluminum pots and pans could cause Alzheimer's. Not so: Aluminum cookware is perfectly safe.

➤ **Aluminum.** Too much aluminum can cause nerve and brain damage. The average person doesn't need to worry much about this, but if you're a heavy user of aluminum-based antacids you could have a problem.

➤ **Arsenic.** Believe or not, you actually need this in very, very small amounts. Most people get about 140 mcg a day from their food. Doses larger than 250 mcg a day are toxic.

➤ **Cadmium.** Your body doesn't have any known use for cadmium, so it's never developed a way to get rid of it. Unfortunately, cadmium is found in cigarette smoke and air pollution, so you could accumulate a toxic amount over many years. If you don't already have enough good reasons to stop smoking, cadmium is another.

➤ **Lead.** This stuff is really bad for you, even though your body normally has a tiny amount of it. Even small amounts of extra lead can cause nerve damage, anemia, mental impairment, and muscle weakness. Recent research also ties lead exposure to high blood pressure. Most cases of lead poisoning occur from exposure to lead-based paint and air pollution. Young children are especially at risk.

➤ **Mercury.** This is another mineral that you have naturally in very small amounts. In larger amounts, though, it can do real damage and should be avoided. Mercury is used in a lot of industrial processes, so it can end up in air and water pollution. Fish such as tuna and swordfish that swim in mercury-contaminated water and eat smaller fish also contaminated with mercury may accumulate high levels of it. If you then eat the fish, you'll also get the mercury that's in it. Experts suggest eating these fish no more than once a week—less if you're pregnant or breast-feeding. What about the mercury in your silver dental fillings? We're not sure if this is really dangerous or not—talk to your dentist.

How can you avoid all these dangerous minerals? To a degree, you can't in our industrial society. There are some simple steps you can take though: have lead paint removed, stop smoking, and avoid contaminated food, water, and air.

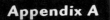

Appendix A

Glossary

antioxidant enzymes   These enzymes protect your body by capturing free radicals and, in a complex series of steps, escorting them out of your body before they do any additional damage.

atherosclerosis   Medical term for hardening of the arteries. Atherosclerosis starts with fatty deposits called atheromas in your arteries. The atheroma slowly gets bigger and harder and turns into a waxy substance called plaque. The plaque narrows or even blocks the artery.

benign prostatic hypertrophy (BPH)   A small male organ called the prostate gland wraps around the urethra, the tube that carries urine from your kidneys to your bladder. As males get older (especially when over age 50), the prostate may enlarge and start pressing on the urethra, a condition called benign prostatic hypertrophy (BPH). The main symptom is the need to urinate frequently.

cardiac arrhythmias   Make your heart beat irregularly. Sometimes the arrhythmia makes you have an extra heartbeat or skip one; it could also make your heart beat too fast. Cardiac arrhythmias can be serious. See your doctor at once if you're having symptoms.

carotenes   Natural pigments in red, orange, and yellow plant foods (cantaloupes, carrots, and tomatoes) and in potatoes and dark-green leafy vegetables. The name comes from carrots. Because your body has to change the carotenes into vitamin A before you can use them, carotenes are sometimes called precursor vitamin A or provitamin A.

clotting factors   Substances in your blood that help it clot and stop bleeding. You make a lot of different clotting factors, but the most important is prothrombin. You need vitamin K to make prothrombin and several other clotting factors.

cobalamin   Another name for vitamin B_{12}. To absorb cobalamin from your food, your stomach naturally secretes a special substance called intrinsic factor. Without it, you can't absorb the cobalamin.

collagen   A protein that makes up the connective tissue that holds your cells together and makes up your bones, tendons, muscles, teeth, skin, blood vessels, and every other part of you.

diuretic   Diuretic drugs make your kidneys produce more urine, which removes water—and also some minerals and vitamins—from your body. Prescription diuretics such as furosemide (Lasix®) are mostly used to treat high blood pressure. These drugs don't usually lower your magnesium level, although they may affect your potassium level.

enzymes   Chemical compounds your body makes from various combinations of proteins, vitamins, and minerals. Enzymes speed up chemical reactions in your body.

epithelial tissues   These tissues cover the internal and external surfaces of your body. Since your skin covers all of your outside, it's one giant external epithelial tissue. Epithelial tissue also lines your nose and your eyes. Your entire digestive tract is lined with epithelial tissue. So are your lungs and your urinary and reproductive tracts.

ergocalciferol   The vitamin D you get from foods or supplements is called vitamin D$_2$ or ergocalciferol. The *ergo-* comes from ergot, a fungus that grows on rye plants. Substances in ergot cause hallucinations—LSD was first made from ergot. Although vitamin D was discovered in ergot, your daily supplement is made from yeast or fish liver and can't cause hallucinations.

fortified milk   Has vitamin D and (sometimes) vitamin A added. In the 1930s milk producers began adding 400 IU to every quart in an effort to eliminate rickets, a disease caused by a crippling shortage of vitamin D. Without it, bones can't absorb enough calcium to grow straight and strong.

free radicals   Unstable oxygen atoms created by your body's natural processes and the effects of toxins such as cigarette smoke. Free radicals, especially singlet oxygen and hydroxyl, cause damage to your cells, but they're not all bad. You use free radicals as part of your immune system to defend against invading bacteria.

hemoglobin   The oxygen-carrying protein that gives your red blood cells their color. Every molecule of hemoglobin has four atoms of iron in it.

hormones   Chemical messengers your body makes to tell your organs what to do. Hormones regulate many activities, including your growth, blood pressure, heart rate, glucose levels, and sexual characteristics.

neural tube defect (NTD)   This defect occurs when the growing brain, spinal cord, and vertebrae (the bones of the spine) of an unborn baby don't develop properly during the first month of pregnancy.

osteoporosis A disease in which bones break easily because they are thin, porous, and brittle. Osteoporosis has several related causes, but too little calcium in the diet plays a big part in causing it.

thiamin pyrophosphate (called **TPP** for short) An enzyme your body needs to convert carbohydrates into energy. You need thiamin to make it—no other B vitamin can.

thymus Your thymus gland is a small organ in your neck just above your breastbone. It makes some of the hormones that tell your immune system what to do. When you're born, your thymus is quite large. By the time you're 40, it's shrunk. Recent studies show that zinc can revitalize your thymus and get it working again.

thyroid A small butterfly shaped gland found in your neck just below your Adam's apple. It produces hormones, including one called thyroxin that regulates your metabolism. A shortage of iodine can lead to hypothryoidism, or underactive thyroid. When that happens, your thyroid gland swells up and forms a lump called a goiter in your neck.

tocopherol Another name for vitamin E. In 1922, researchers found that lab rats on a diet of highly processed foods with no fats couldn't have babies. When the rats were given wheat-germ oil—high in vitamin E—they became fertile again. Vitamin E was originally called tocopherol, from the Greek words *tokos,* meaning "offspring," and *pheros,* meaning "to bear."

tryptophan One of the nine essential amino acids—you can only get it from your food. Your body uses half the tryptophan it gets to help make the thousands of complicated proteins that keep you running. The rest is converted to niacin. The best way to get your tryptophan is through the proteins in your food.

Resources

Finding Nutritionally Oriented Health Care

For help finding nutritionally oriented physicians and other health-care professionals near you, contact:

American Academy of Environmental Medicine
American Financial Center
7701 East Kellogg, Suite 625
Wichita, KS 67207
316-684-5500
www.healthy.net/pan/pa/NaturalTherapies/aaem

American Chiropractic Association
Council on Nutrition
1701 Clarendon Boulevard
Arlington, VA 22209
800-986-4636
www.amerchiro.org

American College for Advancement in Medicine
23121 Verdugo Drive, Suite 204
Laguna Hills, CA 92653
800-532-3688
www.acam.org

American Holistic Medical Association
4101 Lake Boone Trail, Suite 201
Raleigh, NC 27607
703-556-9245
www.holisticmedicine.org

Foundation for the Advancement of Innovative Medicine (FAIM)
Two Executive Boulevard, Suite 204
Suffern, NY 10901
914-368-9797

For more information about healthy eating or to find a qualified professional nutritionist near you, contact:

American Dietetic Association
216 West Jackson Boulevard
Chicago, IL 60606
800-877-1600
ADA nutrition hotline: 800-366-1655
www.eatright.org

International and American Associations of Clinical Nutritionists
5200 Keller Springs Road, Suite 410
Dallas, TX 75248
972-250-2829
www.iaacn.org

Useful Nutrition Web Sites
Arbor Nutrition Guide
www.arborcom.com

Tufts University Nutrition Navigator
www.navigator.tufts.edu

U.S. Department of Agriculture Food and Nutrition
Information Center
www.nal.usda.gov/fnic

Supplement Information and Regulation

General Information

For more information about nutritional supplements in
general:

Council for Responsible Nutrition
1875 Eye Street NW, Suite 400
Washington, DC 20006
202-872-1488
www.crnusa.org

For more information about alternative and complementary medicine, including nutrition:

**National Center for Complementary and Alternative
Medicine**
National Institutes of Health
NCCAM Clearinghouse
Box 8218
Silver Spring, MD 20907
888-644-6226
nccam.nih.gov

Federal Regulations

U.S. Department of Health and Human Services
Food and Drug Administration (FDA)
5600 Fishers Lane
Rockville, MD 20857
888-INFO FDA
www.fda.gov

Industry Standards
National Nutritional Foods Association (NNFA)
3931 MacArthur Boulevard, Suite 101
Newport Beach, CA 92660
800-966-6632
www.nnfa.org

Eating Your Vitamins and Minerals

What's the best way to get your daily dose of the vitamins and minerals you need? Eat them, through a varied diet rich in fresh fruits and vegetables, nuts, whole grains, and high-quality protein such as fish, chicken, beef, and dairy products. The following tables gives the top 10 choices for the all the vitamins and the most important minerals.

Vitamin A

Food	Amount	Vitamin A in RE
American cheese	1 oz.	82
beef liver	3 oz.	9,000
butter	1 tsp.	35
cheddar cheese	1 oz.	86
chicken leg	1	45
chicken liver	3$^1/_2$ oz.	4,913
egg	1 large	97
ice cream, vanilla	1 cup	133
milk	1 cup	149
swordfish	3 oz.	101

Beta Carotene

Food	Amount	Beta Carotene in IU
broccoli, cooked	1/2 cup	1,940
cantaloupe	1 cup	2,720
carrot, raw	1 medium	8,100
collard greens, cooked	1/2 cup	7,410
pepper, sweet red	1/2 cup	2,225
spinach, cooked	1/2 cup	7,290
squash, winter	1/2 cup	6,560
sweet potato, cooked	1 medium	9,230
tomato	1 medium	1,110
turnip greens, cooked	1/2 cup	4,570

Thiamin

Food	Amount	Thiamin in mg
beef liver	3 oz.	0.23
black beans	1/2 cup	0.21
ham	3 oz.	0.82
oatmeal	1 cup	0.26
peanuts	3 oz.	0.36
pecans	3 oz.	0.27
potato	1 medium	0.22
rice, brown	1 cup	0.20
sunflower seeds	3 oz.	1.95
wheat germ	1/4 cup	0.55

Riboflavin

Food	Amount	Riboflavin in mg
almonds	1 oz.	0.22
beef liver	3 oz.	3.60
cottage cheese, low-fat	1 cup	0.42
egg	1 large	0.26
milk, low-fat	1 cup	0.52
mushrooms, cooked	1/2 cup	0.23
pork, roasted	3 oz.	0.30
tuna, fresh	3 oz.	0.26
wheat germ	1/4 cup	0.55
yogurt, low-fat	8 oz.	0.49

Niacin

Food	Amount	Niacin in mg
beef, ground	3 oz.	4.0
beef liver	3 oz.	10.0
chicken breast	3 oz.	8.5
mushrooms, cooked	1/2 cup	3.5
peanut butter	2 Tbsp.	3.8
peanuts	1 oz.	3.8
pork, roasted	3 oz.	5.5
salmon, canned	3 oz.	5.0
tuna, canned in water	3 oz.	11.3
turkey breast	3 oz.	8.5

Pyridoxine

Food	Amount	Pyridoxine in mg
avocado	1/2 medium	0.40
banana	1 medium	0.66
beef liver	3 oz.	0.78
chicken breast	3 oz.	0.34
lentils	1 cup	0.35
navy beans	1 cup	0.30
pork, roasted	3 oz.	0.39
potato, baked	1 medium	0.70
tuna, canned in water	3 oz.	0.30
wheat germ	1/4 cup	0.38

Folic Acid

Food	Amount	Folic Acid in mcg
asparagus	1/2 cup	132
black beans	1 cup	256
black-eyed peas	1 cup	123
chick peas	1 cup	282
kidney beans	1 cup	229
lentils	1 cup	358
lima beans	1 cup	273
liver, chicken	3 oz.	660
navy beans	1 cup	255
spinach, cooked	1/2 cup	131

Cobalamin

Food	Amount	Cobalamin in mcg
beef, ground	3 oz.	2.10
beef liver	3 oz.	68.00
chicken liver	3 oz.	16.60
clams, canned	3 oz.	84.06
cottage cheese, low-fat	1 cup	1.43
egg	1 large	0.77
flounder	3 oz.	2.13
liverwurst	1 slice	2.42
pâté de foie gras	1 oz.	2.66
tuna, light, in water	3 oz.	2.54

Pantothenic Acid

Food	Amount	Pantothenic Acid in mg
beef liver	3 oz.	3.90
chicken leg	1 medium	0.63
chicken liver	3 oz.	4.63
chick peas	1 cup	0.72
lentils	1 cup	1.26
mushrooms, cooked	1/2 cup	1.69
oatmeal	1 cup	0.47
potato, baked	1 medium	1.12
tuna, canned in water	3 oz.	3.00
yogurt, low-fat	1 cup	1.34

Vitamin C

Food	Amount	Vitamin C in mg
broccoli, cooked	1/2 cup	58
grapefruit, pink	1/2 medium	47
guava	1 medium	165
kiwi	1 medium	75
lemon	1 medium	31
mango	1 medium	57
orange, navel	1 medium	80
orange juice, fresh	1 cup	97
papaya	1 medium	188
strawberries	1 cup	85

Vitamin D

Food	Amount	Vitamin D in IU
cod-liver oil	1 tsp.	460
egg	1 large	25
herring, fresh	3 oz.	270
liver, beef	3 oz.	26
mackerel, fresh	3 oz.	943
margarine	1 Tbsp.	21
milk	8 oz.	100
salmon, fresh	3 oz.	350
sardines, canned	3 oz.	1,000
shrimp	3 oz.	129

Vitamin E

Food	Amount	Vitamin E in mg
almonds	1 oz.	6.72
avocado	1/2 medium	2.32
peanut butter	2 Tbsp.	3.00
peanuts	1 oz.	2.56
safflower oil	1 Tbsp.	4.60
sunflower oil	1 Tbsp.	6.30
sunflower seeds	1 oz.	14.18
sweet potato	1 medium	5.93
wheat germ	1/4 cup	4.08
wheat-germ oil	1 Tbsp.	20.30

Vitamin K

Food	Amount	Vitamin K in mcg
broccoli, raw	1/2 cup	58
cabbage, raw	1/2 cup	52
cauliflower, raw	1/2 cup	96
egg	1 large	25
soybean oil	1 Tbsp.	76
spinach, raw	1/2 cup	74
strawberries	1 cup	21
tomato, raw	1 medium	28
turnip greens, raw	1/2 cup	182
wheat germ	1 oz.	10

Calcium

Food	Amount	Calcium in mg
American cheese	1 oz.	124
cheddar cheese	1 oz.	204
cottage cheese, low-fat	1 cup	138
milk	8 oz.	300
mozzarella cheese	1 oz.	147
navy beans	1 cup	128
salmon (with bones)	3 oz.	203
Swiss cheese	1 oz.	219
tofu, uncooked	$1/2$ cup	130
yogurt, plain low-fat	8 oz.	415

Iron

Food	Amount	Iron in mg
black beans	1 cup	3.6
chick peas	1 cup	3.2
kidney beans	1 cup	3.2
liver, beef	3 oz.	5.8
liver, chicken	3 oz.	7.3
molasses, blackstrap	1 Tbsp.	3.5
potato, baked	1 medium	2.7
raisins, seedless	$2/3$ cup	2.1
spinach, cooked	$1/2$ cup	3.2
white beans	1 cup	6.6

Magnesium

Food	Amount	Magnesium in mg
almonds	1 oz.	86
black beans	1 cup	121
kidney beans	1 cup	80
lentils	1 cup	71
lima beans	1 cup	82
peanut butter	2 Tbsp.	51
spinach, cooked	$1/2$ cup	79
Swiss chard	$1/2$ cup	76
tofu	$1/2$ cup	118
white beans	1 cup	113

Potassium

Food	Amount	Potassium in mg
avocado	$1/2$ medium	550
banana	1 medium	451
black beans	1 cup	801
cantaloupe	1 cup	494
kidney beans	1 cup	713
lentils	1 cup	731
orange juice	8 oz.	474
potato, baked	1 medium	844
prune juice	8 oz.	706
tomato juice	6 oz.	658

Zinc

Food	Amount	Zinc in mg
beef, ground	3 oz.	4.6
beef liver	3 oz.	5.2
cashews	1 oz.	1.6
chick peas	1 cup	2.5
kidney beans	1 cup	1.9
lentils	1 cup	2.5
oysters, raw	6 medium	76.4
wheat germ	$1/4$ cup	3.6
white beans	1 cup	2.5
yogurt	8 oz.	2.0

Index

U-V